REPORT

ON THE

VITAL STATISTICS

OF THE

UNITED STATES,

MADE TO THE

MUTUAL LIFE INSURANCE COMPANY OF NEW YORK.

BY JAMES WYNNE, M. D.,

MEMBER OF THE AMERICAN MEDICAL ASSOCIATION; OF THE AMERICAN ASSOCIATION FOR THE ADVANCEMENT OF SCIENCE; CORRESPONDING MEMBER OF THE AMERICAN ETHNOLOGICAL SOCIETY; OF THE NEW YORK LYCEUM OF NATURAL HISTORY, &c., &c., &c.

NEW YORK: H. BAILLIERE, 290 Broadway.
LONDON: 219 Regent Street.   PARIS: J. B. BAILLIERE ET FILS, Rue Hautefeuille.
MADRID: C. BAILLY BAILLIERE, 11 Calle del Principe.

1857.

PREFACE.

The accompanying Report was originally made to the President and Trustees of the Mutual Life Insurance Company, of New York, who, in the prosecution of an extended business, had long felt the necessity for a more full and exact knowledge of Vital Statistics upon which to base their operations than was attainable. They had, indeed, through their medical examiners and other officials obtained many valuable statistics from all parts of the Union, which, upon the selection of the writer to make this report, were placed by Mr. WINSTON, the President of the Company, under whose auspices they were collected, in his hands, and together furnish no inconsiderable source of information.

The statistical records of the General and State Governments, and the contributions of many individual statisticians, have likewise supplied reliable data, of whose value the reader will have an opportunity of determining for himself. The deductions drawn either from admitted or supposed premises, are so given as to enable a comparison to be instituted between the facts upon which they are based, and the reasoning consequent upon them; and while all mere speculations are avoided, it is hoped that the principles developed may be found a safe guide in the conduct of a business which involves a trust, so vast in a pecuniary point of view, and so sacred in its moral obligations, as that of Life Assurance.

It may be proper to add, that the collection of Vital Statistics, upon a comprehensive scale, is a new subject in the United States; and although this Report embraces many points whose elucidation is tolerably well defined, yet a large number await the collection of those facts which the General or State Governments, or both, must sooner or later gather together.

It is highly gratifying to be able to state in this connection, that in addition to the Company to whom the Report was originally made, all the Life Insurance Companies in the United States, with the exception of six or eight, have, with great unanimity and much kind feeling, united in defraying the expenses of the present publication. This is the more pleasing to the writer, inasmuch as it not only evinces a desire on the part of those engaged in this important and highly intellectual department of business to secure the aid of science, but is at the same time an earnest that, in their esteem, his labors are not devoid of value.

PREFACE.

The Companies above alluded to are—

> NEW YORK LIFE INSURANCE COMPANY, of New York.
> UNITED STATES LIFE INSURANCE COMPANY, of New York.
> THE MANHATTAN LIFE INSURANCE COMPANY, of New York.
> KNICKERBOCKER LIFE INSURANCE COMPANY, of New York.
> MUTUAL BENEFIT LIFE INSURANCE COMPANY, of New Jersey.
> PENN LIFE INSURANCE COMPANY, of Philadelphia.
> UNITED STATES LIFE INSURANCE, ANNUITY AND TRUST COMPANY, of Philadelphia.
> AMERICAN LIFE INSURANCE AND TRUST COMPANY, of Philadelphia.
> MASSACHUSETTS HOSPITAL LIFE INSURANCE COMPANY, of Boston.
> NEW ENGLAND MUTUAL LIFE INSURANCE COMPANY, of Boston.
> UNION MUTUAL LIFE INSURANCE COMPANY, of Boston.
> THE STATE MUTUAL LIFE ASSURANCE COMPANY, of Worcester, Mass.
> CHARTER OAK LIFE INSURANCE COMPANY, of Hartford.
> AMERICAN TEMPERANCE LIFE INSURANCE COMPANY, of Hartford.
> CONNECTICUT MUTUAL LIFE INSURANCE COMPANY, of Hartford.
> INTERNATIONAL LIFE INSURANCE COMPANY, of London.
> LIVERPOOL AND LONDON LIFE INSURANCE COMPANY.

VITAL STATISTICS.

CHAPTER I.

INTRODUCTORY REMARKS.

By a wise provision of Providence, the period of death in any individual instance during a state of health, is always a subject of extreme uncertainty, and it consequently happens that, although human life has an expectation of continuance proportioned to its past duration, and the collateral circumstances by which it is surrounded, yet the span of its existence is liable to be severed at any one moment of its being.

Were the circumstances affecting its duration always the same, the period of life in any particular case might be defined with much certainty; but as these are found to be ever varying, so the expectation inseparably interwoven with them, becomes a question whose solution depends in a great degree upon the doctrine of probability.

It is impossible to determine whether any coming event will happen or not. Yet it is possible to conjecture the number of cases in which it may occur, and of these, the number in which its occurrence is probable. Mathematically speaking the probability of an event, is the ratio of the favorable circumstances likely to occur in its regard, and the proportion of those in which it is likely to happen to those in which it is not; thus, the probability of throwing an ace with dice, is one in six. And again; when two dice are thrown, the probability of any given number being uppermost, as seven is likewise one in six; because, every one of the six numbers on one of the dice may combine with one of the six on the other so as to form the number seven; now, as the number of combinations is thirty-six, and there are six ways in which seven may occur, its chances of occurrence are six in thirty-six times, or one chance in six.

The value of the information thus obtained is far from being lessened because of its dependence upon what at first sight appears to be vague and uncertain. How much the acquired knowledge possessed by mankind is exclusively due to this source, may not at first view be imagined. Upon it are based the actions and judgments which constitute the affairs of every day life—confidence in the succession of future events, and in part, at least, the almost miraculous power, by which the astronomer, following with his calculations the flight of the comet, long after it has disappeared from the field of his telescope—predicts the time of its re-appearance after a fixed and stated interval.

But the problems of the mathematician used in these determinations are the mere instruments, delicate and polished though they may be, by which these questions are determined. The materials from which he fashions his work, are furnished by those statistical records of the movements of population—which enlightened governments have found it to their interest to collect and preserve; and here the researches of medicine become so intimately blended with those of mathematics, that their division is next to impossible, and seems to require that the prosecutor of the one should also be a proficient in the other.

The practice of registering births and deaths, is of extremely antique origin. We are possessed of sufficient information in relation to the habits of the early inhabitants of Asia and Africa, to enable us to speak positively in regard to the fact that, among the more influential and polished nations of these countries, registers of this kind were kept. The practice was continued by the Greeks and the Romans, but the records which contained the enumerations like those of the nations that preceded them, have unfortunately been destroyed; and their previous existence is only revealed by collateral testimony.

The earliest continuous register of births, deaths, and marriages now extant, is that kept by the city of Geneva, in Switzerland, which dates back to 1549, and has been continued from that time to the present, with great care and accuracy. This city, which has attained to a high degree of refinement, furnishes in the improvement in the progression of its population and increased duration of life, a striking evidence in favor of the benefits of the adoption of this system.

I have before me (remarks Mr. Shattuck) the results of an examination made by Edward Mallet, a very able work, published in the "Annales D'Hygiene." From this work it appears that human life has wonderfully improved since these registers were kept. The number of years which it was probable that every individual born would live, appears in the different periods as follows:—

Period.	Years.	Months.	Days.	Rate of Increase.
1550 to 1600	8	7	26	100
1600 to 1700	13	3	16	153
1701 to 1750	27	9	13	321
1751 to 1800	31	3	5	361
1801 to 1813	40	8	10	470
1814 to 1833	45	0	29	521

Showing that the mean duration of life has increased more than five times during these periods!

The progression of the population and increased duration of life has been attended by a progression in happiness. As prosperity advanced, marriages became fewer and later. The proportion of births was reduced, but a greater number of the infants born were preserved, and the proportion of the population in manhood became greater. In the early ages, the excessive mortality was accompanied by an excessive fecundity. In the last ten years of the 17th century, a marriage still produced more than five children; the probable duration of life attained was not 20 years. Towards the end of the 18th century, there were scarcely three children to a marriage, and the probabilities exceeded 32 years. At the present time a marriage only produces 2¾ children, and the probability of life is 45 years.

Geneva has arrived at a high state of civilization. The real productive power of the population has increased in a much greater proportion than the increase in its actual number. The absolute number of the population has only doubled during three centuries; but the value of the population—the productive powers—has more than doubled upon the mere numerical increase. In other words, a population of 27,000, in which the probability of life is 40 years for each individual, is more than twice as strong for the purposes of production, as a population of 27,000, in which the probability or value of life was only 20 years for each individual.

This wonderful improvement is attributed, among other things, by M. Mallet, to the information obtained, rendering the science of public health better known and understood; to larger, better and cleaner dwellings; to more abundant and more healthy food; and to a better regulated public and private life. He cites an instance of the effects of regimen in the preservation of life, where 86 orphans had been reared in one establishment in 24 years, and one only of whom had died. They were taken from the poor, among whom the average mortality was six times as great.

Most of the countries of Europe have systems of registration, more or less perfect; the oldest of which, however, do not extend back to a period beyond eighty years. That of England, which has been productive of more important results than any other, dates from 1838, and is, consequently, of less than twenty years' duration.

In the United States, although some laws were enacted in the New England States at an early period, yet no decisive action was taken until 1842, when Massachusetts, adopting in a great degree the plan of the English Registration Act, had the honor to furnish the nucleus, around which the registration system, so far as it has been adopted, has gathered. An Act for registration was enacted in New York, in 1847; in New Jersey and Connecticut, in 1848; in New Hampshire, in 1849; in Rhode Island, in 1850; in Pennsylvania, Virginia and Kentucky, in 1851; and in South Carolina, in 1853. The results of these various Acts, so far as they have been made public, are to be found in the Annual Registration Reports of Massachusetts, Connecticut, New Jersey, Pennsylvania, Rhode Island, Kentucky and Virginia. Some of these reports, and particularly those of the State of Massachusetts, are prepared with much ability, and constitute valuable contributions to vital statistics. Others, as those of Connecticut, are meagre, and less reliable.

The wide difference manifest in the general character and value of the reports already made, clearly establishes the fact that the United States never can possess a system of registration which will correspond in uniformity and value with those of the Governments of Europe, until the task and responsibility of executing it be confided to the General Government.

What value is attached to this information by the enlightened statesmen of other countries, may be deduced from the following remarks made by the Registrar-General of England:—"The census has been taken decennially with great regularity in the United States of America; and the ages are properly distinguished, but abstracts of the registers of deaths have only been published by the cities of New York, Philadelphia, Boston, and some of the more advanced towns where property has accumulated; and life is watched over with more care and facility than in the back settlements—scantily peopled with a fluctuating population. No correct life-table can, therefore, be formed for the population of America until they adopt, in addition to the census, the system of registration which exists in European States."

" Since an English life-table has now been framed from the necessary data, I venture to express a hope, that the facts may be collected and abstracted, from which life-tables for other countries can be constructed. A comparison of the duration of successive generations in England, France, Prussia, Austria, Russia, America, and other states, would throw much light on the physical condition of the respective populations, and suggest to scientific and benevolent individuals in every country—and to governments—many ways of diminishing the sufferings, and ameliorating the health and condition of the people; for the longer life of a nation denotes more than it does in an individual—a happier life—a life more exempt from sickness and infirmity—a life of greater energy and industry—of greater experience and wisdom. By these comparisons a noble national emulation might be excited; and rival nations would read of sickness diminished, deformity banished, life saved—of victories over death and the grave, with as much enthusiasm as of victories over each other's armies in the field; and the triumph of one would not be the humiliation of the other, for in this contention none could lose territory, or honor, or blood, but all would gain strength."*

In addition to the information collected under the Registration Laws, are the bills of mortality kept by most of the populous towns in the United States. This latter source of information is, at the present moment, so far as it goes, the most reliable; and were it on a sufficiently extended scale, might supersede the necessity for registration, as it obtains under the present State enactments; but it could never equal in exactness and value such a system as is in use in England, were it extended to the whole country, and placed under the control and management of the General Government.

The census mortality returns, although far short of what could be desired, clearly show the ability of the government, under a proper regulated

---

* Fifth Annual Report Register-General of England, p. 19.

system, to collect and arrange mortuary registers, which shall equal in exactness and value, those of any country in Europe. In order to accomplish this, or even to give the ordinary census returns an approximation to correctness, it is necessary that the office work be executed by those who, from peculiar adaptation and long experience, possess an especial fitness for the undertaking.

"Unless there is machinery in advance at the seat of Government, no census can ever be properly taken and published. There is a peculiar education required for these labors which neither comes from zeal or genius, but is the result only of experience. They are the most irksome and trying imaginable, requiring inexhaustible patience and endurance, and baffling almost every effort after accuracy. Long familiarity can alone secure system, economy, and certainty of result. This office machinery exists in all European countries where statistics are the most reliable, but there has been none of it in the United States. Each census has taken care of itself. Every ten years some one at Washington will enter the hall of a department, appoint fifty or a hundred persons under him, who, perhaps, have never compiled a table before, and are incapable of combining a column of figures correctly. Hundreds of thousands of pages of returns are placed in the hands of such persons to be digested. If any are qualified, it is no merit of the system. In 1840, returns were given out by the job to whoever would take them. In 1850, such was the pressure of work, that almost any one could at times have had a desk. Contrast this with the English system, and reflect that one individual presided over the census of 1801, '11, '21 and '31. In Washington, as soon as an office acquires familiarity with statistics, and is educated to accuracy and activity, it is disbanded, and even the best qualified employee is suffered to depart. The government may rely upon paying heavily for the experience which is being acquired. Even the head of the office, whatever his previous training, must expect, if faithful, to learn daily; and it is not going too far to say that a matter of one or two hundred thousand dollars is the difference between the amount which a census would cost, conducted by an office which has had the experience of a previous one, (even if partly or entirely in new hands, which might often be desirable, since the machinery, as in other offices, would be kept up,) and an office without such experience. This can be demonstrated if required. Half of that amount would sustain an office of several persons from census to census, and defray all of the expenses of an annual or biennial report after the closing of the regular one, which itself would be executed with despatch, with greatly less force, and with a more economical and wiser application of labor. The permanent force would have no other interest than the prompt execution of the work."

In regard to the confidence to be reposed in the present mortality returns, the report makes the following candid statement:—

"The federal census of 1850 furnishes the first instance of an attempt to obtain the mortality during one year in all the States of the Union, and had there been as much care observed in the execution of the law as was taken in framing it, and in the preparation of necessary blanks, a mass of information must have resulted relating to the sanitary condition of the country, attained as yet in no other part of the world. This, however, would have been expecting too much. It was to take for granted, first, that the person interrogated in each family, whoever he might be, with regard to its affairs, would be able to recollect whatever death had occurred in it within the period of twelve months; and, second, to give the true designation of the cause of such death. One would think it not unreasonable that the facts of actual deaths would be striking and impressive enough in every household to be remembered for a much longer period than a single year; yet the returns of the marshals have only to be examined with care, and deductions made from them, to satisfy the most careful observer that in the Union at large at least one-fourth of the whole number of deaths have not been reported at all. Making allowance for even this error, the United States would appear to be one of the healthiest countries of which there is any record. The varying ratios between the States, as drawn from the returns, show not so much in favor of or against the health of either, as they do, in all probability, a more or less perfect report of the marshals. Thus it is impossible to believe Mississippi a healthier State than Rhode Island, etc. For *rural* population the returns are no doubt nearer correct than they are for *urban*, and the old States are in general better reported than the new. So far as the educated are in question, the assigned causes of death on the returns, may be considered sufficiently near the truth for popular purposes, though falling far short of the precision necessary in skillful scientific calculations; but among the large mass of the community, vagueness and inaccuracy may naturally be expected, even where the parties are disposed to speak the truth and make the best effort to do so. The physician's certificate of the *cause* of death is the only positively reliable evidence of the fact.

"The other points and particulars of inquiry, such as the age, sex, color, condition, occupation and nativities of parties, the season of decease and duration of sickness, stand upon somewhat different ground, and are, from their character, no doubt as correctly answered as the inquiries of the census relating to the ages, pursuits, etc., of the living.

"Upon the whole, then, and we cannot be too emphatic on this point, whilst this publication of the mortality statistics of the census is disclaimed as of authority in showing the respective pretentions to healthfulness or the degree of unhealthfulness of the several States, or of very great scientific worth in showing the *specific* causes of death, it may be considered of much value, notwithstanding, in giving with even ordinary claims to precision very minute phenomena relating to the deaths of about one-third of a million of people scattered over three millions of square miles of territory. The value of such a multitude of facts cannot but be very great, even although they do not constitute the whole of them. We are every day accustomed to draw deductions for the whole from a part, and to argue out the true and complete from the approximate and uncertain.

"It may also be said in favor of the returns as published, that they constitute but a beginning, and are not, perhaps, further from the truth than were the first attempts in States having registration systems. The same improvement as in these States may be expected hereafter. The publication of this volume will stimulate investigation and lead to a better understanding of the importance of the subject."

CHAPTER II.

TERRITORIAL LIMITS.

The territory embraced within the present limits of the United States extends from N. latitude 29° to 49°, and from the Atlantic to the Pacific Oceans. This vast area contains two millions, nine hundred and thirty-six thousand, one hundred and sixty-six square miles, and embraces a more extended range of soil and climate than that of any other civilized country upon the globe. The opportunity afforded for marking the effects of difference of climate, temperature, soil and social institutions, upon the same people, is without a parallel, and were the statistical data as exact and reliable as those of the smaller States of Europe, the information would exceed in comprehensivness and value, that of any other country, because more extensive and general in its range, and involving questions of migration and the intermingling of races on a scale unknown elsewhere.

The Alleghany and Rocky Mountain ranges divide the face of the country into the Atlantic plain and slope, which is washed by the Atlantic Ocean, and was the earliest settled portion of the United States, the valley of the Mississippi lying between the Alleghany and Rocky Mountain ranges, watered by the Mississippi river and its tributaries, and the Pacific slope, extending from the Rocky Mountains to the shores of the Pacific Ocean, and embracing the auriferous region of California.

The annexed table gives the area of each great division and ratio to the total area of the United States:

Territory.	Area in sq. miles.	Ratio of area of each slope to total area of U. S.
Pacific slope.	766,002	26.09
Atlantic slope proper.	514,416	17.52
Northern Lake region	112,649	3.83
Gulf region.	325,537	11.09
Atlantic, Lake and Gulf east and west of the Mississippi.	952,602	32.44
Mississippi valley, drained by the Mississippi and its tributaries	1,217,562	41.47
Atlantic, including Northern Lake.	627,065	21.35
Mississippi valley and Gulf or Middle region	1,543,099	52.55
Total.	2,936,166	

This is divided into States and Territories, as follows:—

State or Territory.	Area in sq. miles.	Per cent. of total area.	Rank of States, &c., territorially.	State or Territory.	Area in sq. miles.	Per cent. of total area.	Rank of States, &c., territorially.
Alabama.	50,722	1.73	20	Missouri.	67,380	2.29	11
Arkansas	52,198	1.78	18	Nebraska Territory	335,882	11.44	1
California	155,980	5.32	7	New Hampshire.	9,280	0.32	34
Columbia, District of.	60		40	New Mexico Territory	207,007	7.05	4
Connecticut.	4,674	0.15	37	New York.	47,000	1.60	23
Delaware	2,120	0.07	38	New Jersey.	8,320	0.28	35
Florida	59,268	2.02	13	North Carolina	50,704	1.73	21
Georgia.	58,000	1.98	14	Ohio.	39,964	1.36	27
Illinois	55,405	1.89	16	Oregon Territory.	185,030	6.30	5
Indiana	33,809	1.15	29	Pennsylvania	46,000	1.57	24
Indian Territory (south of Kansas.	71,127	2.42	10	Rhode Island.	1,306	0.04	39
				South Carolina	29,385	1.01	31
Iowa	50,914	1.73	19	Tennessee	45,600	1.55	25
Kansas.	114,798	3.91	9	Texas.	237,504	8.09	3
Kentucky	37,680	1.28	28	Utah Territory	269,170	9.17	2
Louisiana	41,255	1.40	26	Virginia.	61,352	2.10	12
Maine	31,766	1.08	30	Vermont.	10,212	0.35	33
Maryland	11,124	0.38	32	Washington Territory	123,022	4.19	8
Massachusetts.	7,800	0.26	36	Wisconsin	53,924	1.84	17
Michigan	56,243	1.91	15				
Minnesota Territory	166,025	5.65	6	Total.	2,936,166		
Mississippi	47,156	1.61	22				

The interior valley of North America begins within the tropics and terminates with the polar circle, traversing the continent from south to north. Dr. Drake says: " Of the area of this great inter-mountain region it is not easy to speak with any precision. This valley cannot be estimated at less than three-fourths of the continental surface. Its northern half is, however, rendered nearly uninhabitable, by the state of its surface and climate; and, therefore, the portion which presents objects of immediate interest to the medical etiologist, does not exceed three millions of square miles, of which as yet not more than one-third has acquired even a sparse population."

The Rocky Mountains, which constitute the western boundary of the great valley, are a continuation of the Cordilleras of Mexico; and acquire an elevation in some places of fourteen thousand feet. The physician who would understand the true character of the climate of the interior valley from south to north, cannot too strongly fix his attention on this lengthened and elevated chain which effectually cuts it off from the genial influences of the Pacific Ocean, and bestows upon it the characteristics of an inland and peculiar climate, differing altogether from any to be found on the western portion of the European continent.

The entire population, according to the census of 1850, was 23,191,876. The estimated population for each succeeding year to 1860, is as follows:—

Years.	Aggregate.
1851,	23,873,717
1852,	24,575,604
1853,	25,298,126
1854,	26,041,890
1855,	26,807,521
1856,	27,595,662
1857,	28,406,974
1858,	29,242,139
1859,	30,101,857
1860,	30,986,851

AGES OF POPULATION.

The distribution of the population of 1850, among the States and Territories, according to their respective ages, is given in the annexed table:—

STATES AND TERRITORIES.	Under 1 year.	1 and under 5.	5 and under 10.	10 and under 20.	20 and under 50.	50 and under 80.	80 and under 100.	100 and upwards.	Unk'n.
Alabama	20,375	110,668	119,389	193,820	273,717	51,328	2,063	163	100
Arkansas	6,642	31,514	33,480	53,375	74,255	10,328	248	24	31
California	273	1,628	2,300	7,510	77,587	2,795	31	....	673
Columbia, District of	1,319	5,428	6,731	11,725	21,485	4,808	216	7	18
Connecticut	7,646	32,808	39,190	77,486	159,097	51,083	3,212	10	260
Delaware	2,554	10,899	13,071	21,842	34,690	8,076	333	9	58
Florida	2,236	12,371	13,380	19,846	33,041	6,247	243	36	45
Georgia	24,858	129,939	141,835	230,552	312,440	62,955	3,142	221	243
Illinois	26,681	115,479	130,622	206,790	316,670	53,309	1,076	18	795
Indiana	32,296	135,416	157,714	246,200	345,431	69,005	1,988	32	334
Iowa	6,099	28,191	31,016	45,476	70,303	10,884	190	1	54
Kentucky	30,073	133,919	151,829	243,745	346,618	72,377	3,482	157	205
Louisiana	12,232	61,202	65,458	105,098	238,019	34,058	1,196	176	323
Maine	13,995	61,781	74,453	138,768	223,081	66,471	3,787	13	820
Maryland	16,482	69,162	78,269	134,124	229,349	52,995	2,504	131	18
Massachusetts	23,192	90,853	102,797	203,765	451,194	115,027	6,433	19	1,234
Michigan	10,898	49,143	59,576	92,449	155,196	29,683	627	9	123
Mississippi	16,086	88,975	94,355	147,564	221,976	35,244	1,232	140	954
Missouri	23,231	98,947	105,176	167,881	252,760	38,776	973	45	155
New Hampshire	6,111	26,952	33,264	70,095	129,446	47,571	3,473	12	52
New Jersey	13,556	54,828	63,761	110,473	194,149	50,147	2,441	25	175
New York	76,337	327,093	377,605	675,980	1,326,860	298,462	13,256	88	1,713
North Carolina	24,734	117,384	131,841	214,097	300,568	76,179	4,337	249	150
Ohio	56,884	253,442	291,286	475,981	734,741	161,589	5,722	58	626
Pennsylvania	64,331	281,066	318,226	524,540	903,085	210,814	8,474	75	1,175
Rhode Island	3,610	14,106	15,591	30,402	65,725	17,148	943	3	17
South Carolina	15,801	91,417	97,184	161,524	238,845	57,837	3,020	206	2,673
Tennessee	30,151	140,117	157,608	260,517	339,180	71,224	3,548	148	224
Texas	6,194	30,594	32,549	50,657	81,172	10,903	270	39	214
Vermont	6,594	31,055	38,153	70,494	123,512	41,605	2,659	10	38
Virginia	36,308	184,163	208,260	344,407	509,714	130,825	7,210	389	385
Wisconsin	10,424	40,948	42,279	62,801	128,097	20,322	326	2	192
Territories. Minnesota	168	751	721	1,030	3,136	264	7	....	....
Territories. New Mexico	1,233	7,566	8,727	14,048	24,246	5,138	406	40	143
Territories. Oregon	310	1,778	1,873	2,652	6,014	597	5	....	65
Territories. Utah	432	1,744	1,369	2,707	4,448	676	4	....	....
Total	629,446	2,868,327	3,241,268	5,420,421	8,949,797	1,976,700	89,077	2,555	14,285

By a calculation of the ratios of each age, as given in the above table, the following results are obtained:

Age.	Number.	Ratio.	Age.	Number.	Ratio.
Under 1 year old	629,446	2.71	80 and under 100	89,077	.39
1 and under 5	2,868,327	12.37	100 and over	2,555	.01
5 " 20	8,661,689	37.35	Age unknown	14,285	.06
20 " 50	8,949,797	38.59			
50 " 80	1,976,700	8.52	Aggregate population	23,191,876	100.00

This population is composed of the inhabitants who assisted in the formation of the government in 1789, and their descendants—of those who have since emigrated, together with their offspring, and of those who were admitted into the Union, when the territory which they inhabited was annexed, as in the case of Florida, Louisiana, New Mexico, and California. The number from this latter source was at the time of the several admissions comparatively insignificant; that from Louisiana being 77,000; from Florida, 10,000; and from New Mexico and California, 60,000. The increase from this source, by propagation, however, has been such as to constitute a very considerable item in the present population returns. One remarkable feature attending the admission of the inhabitants of Louisiana and of the French west of the Mississippi by the extension of the western boundary of the Union, has been the large number of intermarriages between the French population, and those descended from an English ancestry, born in the Atlantic States.

These geographical divisions into sea-coast, mountain, and inland-valley regions, exercise a considerable influence over the progress of population, but much less than those of high and low latitudes and the differences in social position which obtain in the different States of the Union.

In estimating the movements of population in this country, the confederate character of the government must never be lost sight of. The power reserved by each State to enact its own laws, has given to each part of the Union an individuality which is marked and important. The social influences surrounding the inhabitants of two neighboring States, as Massachusetts and Connecticut, or Virginia and Maryland, may not be very different, but they are widely so between remote parts of the Union.

The stern and rigid habits of the New England Puritans—the substantial and frugal customs of the Hollanders who colonized New York—the careful thrift of the Quakers of Pennsylvania—the generous and hospitable character of the early settlers of Maryland—and the careless and noble traits of the gay cavaliers who settled Virginia, are still manifest among their descendants, modifying their character and affecting, in a very decided manner, the population of their respective States.

These observations apply more especially to the States which skirt the Atlantic, yet they are not without force in those in the great valley of the Mississippi. The migration from State to State has had some influence on the population of every State, and in some instances, as that of New York, has effected so decided a change, as greatly to modify their early characteristics.

"Some reflections upon the future growth of the population of the Union, will not be improper in this place. The facts embraced in the census show a regular diminution in the ratio of total as well as of natural increase from decade to decade, up to 1840, making corrections for the admission of new territory, and the shorter period than ten years included between the census of 1820 and 1830. From the declining per cent. of females and young children, Professor Tucker argues that the natural increase of the population is inversely as its density in all of the States, and that the increase of the whole population, for the decades after 1840, would be 32; 31.3; 30.5; 29.6; 28.6; 27.5 per cent. Should emigration, however, remain as it was then, or be but slightly increased from year to year, the series, he supposed, would be 31.8; 30.9; 30; 29; 27.9; 26.8 per cent. The results upon either series will be here shown, but upon both they fall greatly short of the fact for 1850. The ratio from 1840 to 1850 increased over three per cent., instead of declining as before from the previous decade, a result not to be accounted for by the admission of California, New Mexico, &c.

Years.	Population on first series.	Population on second series.
1850	22,400,000	22,000,000
1860	29,400,000	28,800,000
1870	38,300,000	36,500,000
1880	49,600,000	46,500,000
1890	63,000,000	59,800,000
1900	80,000,000	74,000,000."

[*Compend. U. S. Census*, 1850, *p.* 130.]

This table is based upon the assumption of an increase of population in a geometrical ratio, without an adequate compensation for those causes which are always operating to increase or diminish this ratio, and which are so variable in their character as to elude all fixed geometrical rules.

Could a population be found in which the increase arose solely from births and the decrease of deaths, entirely unaffected by migration, it would be found that the excess of births above that of deaths in each year, would be in a fixed ratio to the number living at the beginning of the year, which progression, with a knowledge of the circumstances affecting the rate of mortality, might be determined; for, if the number of births above that of the deaths, bore an exact ratio to the population living, at any one fixed period, the increase could be measured and its results determined by a process in geometrical progression.

But as there is no country, and probably no part of a country, where the population has remained for any length of time so stationary as to be unaffected by migration, it follows, that in order to make a tolerably near approach to the ratio of increase, the effect of this migration must be taken into consideration; and as it is extremely difficult to determine with any degree of precision, either the numbers or the ages of those who enter or depart, so it is proportionably difficult to fix the rate of increase or decrease for any length of time dependant upon their absence or presence.

Besides, all the facts upon which these tables of the future progress of population are based, have been taken from the movements of the living; whereas, in order to ascertain with any exactness the probable increasing population, it is necessary to determine the numbers and the ages of those who die, as well as of those who survive. The seventh census is the only one that has attempted to supply this last element of calculation.

These returns show an aggregate of 320,023 deaths for the year beginning June 1st, 1849, and ending June 1st, 1850, or one death to every 72.5 inhabitants. The report itself, in estimating the value to be attached to these statistics, supposes that one-fourth of the whole number of deaths which have occurred in the Union during the period of one year prior to the enumeration of 1850, have not been reported. Assuming this as the error, the whole number of deaths reported and not reported would be 400,028, or one death to 58 inhabitants.

The average mortality of the English population for the five years, 1838–42, was 2.207 per cent., or nearly one in forty-five. The following table from the sixth report of the Registrar-General, gives in a condensed form, the rates of mortality of several of the principal European States, including England. The enumeration in this latter country being confined to England and Wales, exhibits a much more favorable standard than it would if Ireland and Scotland were included.

	Year.	Population.	ANNUAL DEATHS.		ANNUAL MORTALITY.	
			Year.	Number.	Per Cent.	Living to 1 Death.
England	1841	15,927,867	1838–42	346,905	2.207	45
France	1841	34,213,929	1838–42	816,840	2.397	42
Prussia	1840	14,928,501	1838–41	392,349	2.658	38
Austria	1840	21,571,594	1839–42	651,239	2.995	33
Russia	1842	49,525,420	1842	1,856,138	3.590	28

—[6*th Registrar-General's Report*, p. xxxix.

A comparison of the mortuary records of the United States, with those of the European countries above enumerated, would lead to the belief that a much larger number of unenumerated deaths had occurred than is presumed by the census reports. Were the arbitrary assumption to be made that the number of unrecorded deaths was equal to one-half, instead of one-fourth, of those recorded, the aggregate number would be 480,080, or one death to 48.31 of the living, which produces a result much more in accordance with those of other countries in which reliable mortuary statistics are kept, than the hypothesis of the census report; and for this reason, and for this alone, is entitled to more confidence.

Prof. Tucker, in his ingenious observations upon the probabilities of life in the United States, has deduced the relative number of deaths, from the returns of the living, with results somewhat corresponding to those just given.

"The details of the census of 1850," remarks Prof. Tucker, "compared with those of the census of 1840, fortunately afford us materials for making this interesting estimate with a near approximation to the truth, as we shall thus see.

" It is clear that the difference between the whole population of 1840, and the part of the population of 1850 over ten years of age, would show the number of deaths in ten years, if the country had neither emigration nor immigration. The emigration, however, is insignificant, and the number of immigrants with their increase, we have now the means of ascertaining. But as our numbers in 1850 were augmented by the accession of Texas, New Mexico, and California, as well as by immigration, the population thus acquired must also be deducted. Having found the mortality of the whole population of 1840, that of those who have since come into existence, and are of course under ten in 1850, will be the subject of separate estimate, for which the census also furnishes materials. Let us now see the result :—

Of the whole population of 1850.................... 23,191,877
The whole number under ten is 6,730,044

The number over ten is 16,461,832

" To ascertain the number of immigrants to be deducted from the 16,461,832, we must ascertain—1. The number of immigrants under ten on the 1st of June, 1850. 2. The number over ten who had died between their arrival and June, 1850. These numbers are exhibited in the following table :—*

	Whole No. of immigrants.	No. of children under ten, when they arrived.	No. of years to June, 1850.	No. of children under ten, June 1, 1850.	No. of deaths, to June 1, 1850.	No. over ten, June 1, 1850.
1840–1	83,504	12,825	9½	642	10,110	72,752
1841–2	101,107	15,166	8½	2,275	11,105	87,727
1842–3	75,159	11,274	7½	2,817	7,299	64,043
1843–4	74,607	11,190	6½	3,916	6,182	65,509
1844–5	102,415	15,362	5½	6,912	7,068	88,435
1845–6	147,051	22,057	4½	12,131	8,167	126,753
1846–7	220,882	33,027	3½	20,867	9,384	190,631
1847–8	296,387	44,450	2½	24,760	9,135	262,492
1848–9	296,938	44,540	1½	37,783	5,215	253,940
1849–50	223,984	33,597	½	22,270	2,357	199,357
	1,622,034	243,488	..	134,373	76,022	1,411,639

" If, then, we deduct from the 16,461,832, the population of 1850 over ten years of age, the number of emigrants over that age equal to 1,411,639, and also the number over ten in the newly acquired territories of Texas, &c., which by computation is about 135,000, the difference will be 14,915,193, which is the number of the survivors of the population of June 1, 1840. As this population was 17,069,453, a deduction of the 14,915,193 survivors shows the number of deaths in ten years to have been 2,154,258, averaging 215,425.8 a year. As in computing the rate of mor-

---

* In the computation of deaths contained in the above table, I have, with some hesitation, allowed a somewhat greater mortality than is warranted in the Carlisle life tables, those of Quetelet, and others, since I have assumed one-tenth of the children of the immigrants to be under one year, which probably greatly over-rates their number at an age when the rate of mortality is far greater than at any other age.

tality the deaths are compared with numbers beginning with 17,069,453, and gradually descending through the ten years to 14,915,193, we must take the medium between those numbers, which is 15,992,324. Now, if this number be divided by the annual deaths, 215,425.8, it will show the average annual mortality to be 1 in 74.2 in that part of the population which is over ten years of age.

" To ascertain the mortality of those under ten, our data are somewhat less precise and satisfactory. Two modes of making the estimate present themselves, which lead to different results; and when we shall have more full and reliable data than at present, truth will probably be found to lie between them.

"*First.*—If we assume that the mortality of the children under ten is the same in the United States as in France, according to their respective numbers—and there is no obvious reason why it should be materially different—then, according to the tables which we owe to the patient labors of Heuschling, the number of deaths of the children under ten in the United States, in 1850, was 224,868, exclusive of the children of immigrants between 1840 and 1850. If to this number we add the deaths of the population over ten, 215,425, we have 440,293 for the whole number of deaths in 1850, which exhibits a mortality of 1 in 43.4.

"*Secondly.*—If, however, we adopt the unsatisfactory data afforded by the seventh census, then we may thus estimate the average mortality. According to that census, the number of white and free colored children who died under one year of age, was 43,055, which it must be recollected included the children of immigrants, with the increase of the population generally, for the year 1850. Let us deduct ten per cent. for this portion; for, though the children of immigrants appear not to have exceeded an 11th or 12th of that class, yet, in consideration of the admitted greater mortality, both of immigrants and their children, 10 per cent. does not seem too much for their proportion of deaths. If to the number, thus reduced to 38,749, we add the number of slaves who die at that early age, 10,481, we shall have 49,230 deaths of children in the first year after their birth.

"What is the number for the other nine years? It may be approximated in this way. The whole number of white persons from 5 to 10 years of age, and from 10 to 15, is 5,106,257, one-tenth of which may be presumed to give the number of those whose age is about ten. If one-tenth of this tenth be deducted (for the children of immigrants,) the remainder, 459,563, will exhibit the number of children ten years old in 1850, of the population of 1840.

"Their annual number of deaths we will assume to be 1 in 120, which assumes a somewhat greater mortality than is estimated at this period of life by the most approved life tables of Europe. This would be 3,998.7 for the annual deaths of the whites of 10 years of age, and 852.2 for those of the colored race, in all 4,852. But as there were 49,230 deaths of both classes in the first year of the decade, and 4,852 in the last, the mean—27,041—gives us the annual average deaths of one-tenth of the children under 10, or 270,410 for the whole number. To this, if we add 215,425 for the deaths of persons over ten, we shall have 485,836 for the annual deaths of the population of 1840, excluding all accessions from foreign sources.

The population of 1850, with that exclusion, is as follows:—

Gross amount 23,191,876
From which deduct the immigrants, with their increase, at
   the rate of 3 per cent. per annum from the time of their
   arrival 1,840,233
Accession from Texas, &c........................ 200,000
                                               ——— 2,040,233
                                                       21,151,643

"The mean between this number and the 17,069,453, the population of 1840, is 19,110,548, which, divided by 485,836, the total number of annual deaths, we have an average mortality in the year of 39.3 for the whole population, white and colored, bond and free."

These deductions are certainly curious, and in the absence of more positive elements of calculation, are entitled to respectful consideration. The number of deaths, as made apparent by the mortality returns, is evidently under-estimated: the extent of the error can only be approximated by the assumption of such data as are supplied by the returns of the living; and although the conclusions derived from this source are by no means beyond question, yet they furnish the best means of correcting the error, at the disposal of the philosophic enquirer.

CHAPTER III.

PRODUCTIVE CAPACITY OF POPULATION.

The extreme rapidity with which the population of this country has increased, has led to the adoption of the popular belief, that because its percentage of increase has exceeded that of any other country, it is consequently the most healthy of all others.

Eminent statisticians, and particularly those of other countries, deducing their results from the living alone, have arrived at a different conclusion. Mr. Chadwick, in his work on the "Pressure and Progress of the Causes of Mortality among Different Classes of the Community," published in 1844, remarks :—

" Notwithstanding the earlier marriages, and the extent of emigration, and the general increase of the population, the whole circumstances appear to me to prove this to be the case of a population depressed to a low age, chiefly by the greater proportionate pressure of the causes of disease and premature mortality. The proportionate numbers at each interval of age, in every 10,000 of the two populations, are as follows :—

	United States of America.	England and Wales.
Under 5 years	1744	1324
5 and under 10	1417	1197
10 " 15	1210	1089
15 " 20	1091	997
20 " 30	1816	1780

			United States of America.	England and Wales.
30 and under		40	1160	1289
40	"	50	732	959
50	"	60	436	645
60	"	70	245	440
70	"	80	113	216
80	"	90	32	59
90 and upwards			4	5
			10,000	10,000
Average age of all the living			22 years 2 months.	26 years 7 months.

"Here it may be observed, that whilst in England there are 5025 persons between 15 and 50, who have 3610 children or persons under 15; in America there are 4789 persons living between 15 and 50 years of age, who have 4371 children dependent upon them. In England there are in every ten thousand persons 1365 who have obtained above 50 years' experience; in America there are only 830.

"The moral consequences of the predominance of the young and passionate in the American community, are attested by observers to be such as have already been described in the General Sanatory Report as characteristic of those crowded, filthy, and badly administered districts in England, where the average duration of life is short, the proportion of the very young great, and the adult generation transient.

"The difference does not arise solely from the greater proportion of children arising from a greater increase of population, though that is to some extent consistent with what has been proved to be the effect of a severe general mortality; the effects of the common cause of depression is observable at each interval of age; the adult population in America is younger than in England, and if the causes of early death were to remain the same, it may be confidently predicted that the American population would remain young for centuries.

	Years.	Months.
The average age of all alive above 15 in America is	33	6
The average age of all alive above 15 years in England and Wales is	37	5
The average age of all above 20 years in America is	37	7
In the whole of England the average of all above 20 years is	41	1."

The average age of the whole population, according to the census of 1840, is correctly given by Mr. Chadwick. The average age of the white population is 22.71 years. The returns of 1850 show an increase of the aggregate age, from Mr. Chadwick's estimate, from 22.16, to that of 22.89 years, and of the white population from 22.71 to 23.10, which, as compared with the previous census, furnishes a highly favorable result:—

Classes.	Average age.
Whites	23.10
Free colored	24.54
Slaves	21.35
Aggregate	22.89

A country whose population is so distributed that the larger proportion of its members are of an age which fits them for active employments, is placed under circumstances the most favorable for advancement. Mr. Shattuck has proposed a division of society into three classes, for the purpose of determining the number of those fitted for employment, and those which are not—those under fifteen years of age he denominates the *dependant class*, because dependant upon others for support; those between fifteen and sixty he calls the *productive class*, because they are in the full possession of their energies, and competent not only to produce a sufficiency for themselves, but likewise for those who are dependant upon them; those above sixty he defines as the *aged class*. With the view of ascertaining the condition of the population as affected by this standard, the following table has been constructed:—

AGE.	WHITES.		FREE COLORED.		SLAVES.		AGGREGATE.	
	Number.	Ratio per ct.	Number.	Ratio per ct.	Number.	Ratio per ct.	Number.	Ratio per ct.
15 years and under	8,002,715	40.93	171,181	39.40	1,455,774	45.43	9,629,670	41.52
Over 15 and under 60	10,720,175	54.83	238,859	54.97	1,630,095	50.87	12,589,129	54.28
60 and over	819,871	4.19	24,169	5.56	114,752	3.58	958,792	4.14
Unknown ages	10,307	.05	286	.07	3,692	.12	14,285	.06
Totals	19,553,068	100.00	434,495	100.00	3,204,313	100.00	23,191,876	100.00

In this, as in the preceding table, an advance in the elements of productiveness are manifest. The productive class of the white population in 1830, was 51.01 per cent., and the burdensome, composed of the young and the aged, 48.99 per cent. In 1840, the productive class was 52.35, and the burdensome, 47.65 per cent.; and in 1850, the former class had increased to 54.83 per cent., while the latter had declined to 45.17 per cent., being an increase of 2.48 per cent. in the productive capacity of the whole population, and a corresponding decline in the ratio of those requiring support. The productive class in England is 56.70 per cent. of the population; and in Sweden, 56.93 per cent., being about two per cent. higher than in the United States.

It is a question whether a larger amount of the results of productiveness may not be evolved, with a less per centage of productive capacity, numerically, for a long consecutive period of years in the United States than in England or Sweden. In both of these countries, as well as in most others, except this, upon which extensive observations have been made, the density of population is such as to require a large proportion of the fruits of the earth garnered each year to maintain the population.

When from any cause the crops fall greatly short of their usual amount, much distress is produced among the laboring population, who depend for their daily supply of food, upon the earnings of their daily labor. The proportion which the rate of wages bears to the necessaries of life being largely diminished by the exaltation of the prices of food, occasioned by the scarcity, the amount of food consumed by the laboring classes is lessened in quantity, and not unfrequently deteriorated in quality.

The effect of a diminished supply of food is to lessen the capacity for labor, and to induce disease. It is consequently found that dysentery, fever, and frequently severe epidemics, are the constant attendants upon short crops in such communities as reside in the more populous countries of the globe.

The failure of the potato crop in Ireland in 1846 and 1847, was followed by one of the most severe visitations of typhus fever which has ever desolated that country.

The Prussian Government, whose registration system is so perfect, as to give a very accurate idea of the movement of its inhabitants, became so much alarmed at the effect of the diminished crop of 1855, as to induce it to order a series of experiments to be made upon Indian Corn, as an article of food, for its humbler population, in the event of the deficiency amounting to a serious inconvenience. This provident act was induced by a full knowledge of the baneful effects of short crops as revealed by the registration system.

The large amount of land under cultivation in the United States, and the abundant harvests invariably secured, furnish to each individual a quantity of food exceeding threefold in amount that used by the average laboring classes on the continent of Europe, and places all thought of a small supply out of the question.

With the exception of some few employments in the more populous cities, labor is always in demand at such remunerative wages as to admit of the purchase of nutritious food, not only in quantities sufficient to sustain life, but to gratify the cravings of the most inordinate appetite. The artizan in town, and the laborer in the country, are supplied each day with a substantial repast of animal and vegetable food. This is a matter of universal occurrence, and extends to every section of the country, and with but few exceptions to each department of industry. These exceptions are to be found principally among the females in populous cities, who gain their livelihood by plain sewing, the manufacture of cheap clothing, and like unremunerative occupations.

" The standard of comfort for the laboring class is much higher here than it is in England, so far as it concerns the consumption of animal food, in consequence of the peculiar circumstances of this country, where the husbandry and useful arts of a cultivated people are conjoined with the thin population of a rude one. In every part of Europe, population and the arts have advanced at the same rate; and the ascertained slowness of the rate supposes straitened means of subsistence in every stage of the progress. This is conclusively proved, as to England, by the fact that her population, which, in 1377, had been 2,350,000, had increased in 1800, that is, in 423 years, only to 8,872,980; since nothing but great difficulty in obtaining the means of subsistence, and extreme discomfort with the great mass of the people, could have retarded the period of duplication with our progenitors to upwards of two hundred years."*

That a population supplied with an abundance of substantial food, is competent to perform a greater amount of labor than a similar population, but illy provided for in this particular, is evident. What is the direct effect upon the physical energies of the population of the United States, produced by this condition of things, can only be ascertained by an accumulation of statistical evidence.

---

* Tucker's Progress of the United States, p. 112.

The employments of the industrial classes furnish a tolerably fair indication of the available labor of a population. With this view, the following summary of the pursuits of the population of the United States is given :—

"Of the free population in 1850, amounting to 19,987,563, the number of males above fifteen years of age who were employed in different branches of industry was 5,371,876. Supposing the number of females, who in their appropriate employments are at least as industrious as the males, to be equal, then the industrious class of both sexes above fifteen amount to 10,743,562. The difference between this number and that of the whole free population is 9,243,811. If from this residue we deduct the tenants of the poor-houses, hospitals, jails, and penitentiaries, the superannuated and the children under fifteen, all of whom are either too young to work, are already employed or qualifying themselves for future employment, the remainder, constituting the voluntary idle and unproductive class, would be an inconsiderable portion of the community, as may be thus seen :—

Whole number, after deducting the working classes		9,243,811
Children under 15 by the census	8,173,896	
Persons over seventy by the same	308,686	
Paupers by the same	50,352	
In hospitals for the insane, blind, &c., by the same	50,994	
In State prisons and penitentiaries, by the same	5,646	
In jails and houses of correction	7,444	
		8,597,018
Whole number of idle class		646,793

"It would thus seem that the whole number of the idle class of both sexes between the ages of fifteen and seventy is less than 3 per cent., or one person in thirty-three of the free population; and though the labor to which man is inevitably destined is occasionally excessive or irksome, yet in the main his bread is sweetened as well as moistened by the sweat with which it is earned :—*

Of these, there are engaged in—

1.	Mental pursuits	179,032 or	3	per cent.
2.	Producers	2,544,777 "	42	"
3.	Manufacturers	1,229,607 "	24	"
4.	Commercial pursuits................	316,053 "	6	"
5.	Miscellaneous.....................	1,102,422 "	19	"
		5,371,876	100	"

---

* Ibid Appendix, p. 44.

CHAPTER IV.

EMIGRATION.

The effect of emigration upon the population of the United States is an important one, and requires especial consideration. The entire foreign population in 1850 was 2,210,839, and its ratio to the white and free colored population, 11.06 per cent., which is thus distributed:—

States and Territories.	Total Foreign.	Per ct. of foreign to white and free col'd population.	States and Territories.	Total Foreign.	Per ct. of foreign to white and free col'd population.
Alabama	7,638	1.78	New Hampshire......	13,571	4.27
Arkansas..............	1,628	1.00	New Jersey...........	58,364	11.93
California.............	22,358	24.15	New York...........	651,801	21.04
Columbia, District of....	4,967	10.35	North Carolina.......	2,524	.43
Connecticut............	37,473	10.11	Ohio................	218,512	11.03
Delaware..............	5,211	5.84	Pennsylvania.........	294,871	12.75
Florida................	2,757	5.73	Rhode Island	23,111	15.66
Georgia................	5,907	1.13	South Carolina	8,662	3.06
Illinois	110,593	12.99	Tennessee	5,740	.75
Indiana................	54,426	5.51	Texas................	16,774	10.86
Iowa	21,232	11.05	Vermont.............	32,831	10.45
Kentucky..............	29,189	3.78	Virginia	22,394	2.36
Louisiana..............	66,413	24.33	Wisconsin	106,695	34.94
Maine.................	31,456	5.39	Terri- ⎧ Minnesota....	2,048	33.70
Maryland..............	53,288	10.82	tories. ⎨ New Mexico .	2,063	3.85
Massachusetts..........	160,909	16.18	⎩ Oregon......	1,159	8.72
Michigan..............	54,852	13.79	Utah	1,990	17.53
Mississippi.............	4,958	1.67			
Missouri	72,474	12.19	Total............	2,210,839	11.06

Of these, 961,719 were born in Ireland; 278,675 in England; 70,550 in Scotland; 29,868 in Wales; 147,711 in British America; 54,069 in France; 10,549 in Prussia; 573,225 in the rest of Germany; 946 in Austria; 13,358 in Switzerland; 12,678 in Norway; 9,848 in Holland; 3,559 in Sweden; 3,113 in Spain; 3,645 in Italy; 5,772 in the West Indies; 1,638 in Denmark; 1,313 in Belgium; 1,414 in Russia; 1,274 in Portugal;

785 in China; 585 in the Sandwich Islands; 13,317 in Mexico; and 1,543 in South America. From this it would appear that the British subjects, born either in Great Britain, Ireland, or British America, who had emigrated to the United States, numbered 1,488,523, and constitute two-thirds of the whole foreign-born population.

In the selection of their residence, the immigrants have manifested a decided preference for some sections of country over others; thus, while in the Middle States they constitute one-fifth of the population, and in the Northern and Eastern a little less than one-eighth, their ratio in the South-western is diminished to one-twentieth, and in the Southern States to one-fiftieth of the whole population.

The two States least affected by foreign emigration are North Carolina and Tennessee; the whole number in the former State being 2,524, and constituting but forty-three hundredths of one per cent. of the entire population; and in the latter 5,740, and making three-fourths of one per cent. of the whole number of inhabitants. In South Carolina, the number of foreign inhabitants is 8,662, and bears a ratio of 3.06 per cent. to the entire population. Of these, 4,643 reside in the city of Charleston, and 4019 in the rural districts, The foreign population of Charleston constitutes 21,28 per cent. of the whole.

Indeed, there appears to be a marked desire on the part of immigrants to select populous cities, rather than rural districts, as a place of residence. The annexed table, showing the proportion of Irish, German and Prussian immigrants residing in the large cities, will develope this proposition:

1850.	In United States.	In large cities.	Ratio per ct. to whole.
Irish	961,719	382,402	39.76
Germans and Prussians	583,774	212,559	36.43

The annexed exhibit of the native and foreign population of the following European States, shows how much more decided the effect of this element is in this country than in Europe:—

	Census.	Whole Population.	Foreign Population.	Per ct. of Foreign Population.
Great Britain and the islands in the British seas..	1851	20,959,477	56,665	0.27
France...	1851	35,783,170	378,563	1.06
Denmark..	1851	1,407,747	13,042	0.43
Sardinia	1848	4,918,855	26,465	0.54
Holland..	1849	3,056,879	70,855	2.32
Belgium	1846	4,337,196	76,479	1.76

Much the largest proportion of emigrants who arrive in the United States are in the most humble circumstances, frequently with constitutions shattered by privation, and with slender means to provide for themselves even the most simple necessaries of life. From early association, aided, perhaps, by the necessity of the moment, they are accustomed to herd together (for they cannot be said to live) in large numbers, in those parts of our populous seaports where rooms are less expensive, and a residence is least desirable.

Surrounded by all the elements of disease which abound in the densely crowded and illy ventilated portions of populous places, the victims of previous privation, and of present want, it might naturally be inferred that the mortality among them would be very great. It unfortunately happens, however, that few bills of mortality are kept in such a manner as to afford a satisfactory solution to this question. Those of New York, and some of the other cities, give the nativity of the persons deceased, and in this manner some clue may be had to the ratio of deaths among the adult population. The mortality returns of Boston and Providence show, that that the mortality among the offspring of the immigrant population, who inhabit large cities, particularly in the earliest period of life, is very great, and far exceeds that which occurs among the native population. Admitting an equality between the immigrant and native population in all other circumstances, than that of the density of their numbers, and the disposition of the former to crowd themselves into an inconceivably small space, and there is left in this source alone a wide disproportion as to the chances of life against the immigrant; for, under like circumstances, the more closely individuals are congregated together, either in their habitations or their persons, the greater is the danger of disease, and the less the probabilities of life. The annexed extract from the North American Review, giving a description of a certain district in Boston, is corroborative of these views:—

"The district selected for comparison comprises Broad, Cove, and Sea streets. These streets are situated near the wharves. They are built principally upon made land, and have numerous blind alleys leading from them. The streets and alleys are badly *drained*, and crowded with an overflowing population. A large number of the houses have no means of sewerage whatever, and all their refuse of every description stagnates about the yards, spreading on every side poisonous exhalations, laden with disease and death. A majority of the houses contain several families, and some of them have no less than nine or ten. Even the cellars of the houses are often inhabited, and in some instances one cellar leads to another, and this to a third, a sort of dungeon, all inhabited by human beings of both sexes and every age. The population of these three streets is 2813, of whom 2738 are foreigners and only 75 Americans. The mortality was *one in 17.6 of the population*, or 5.65 per cent., and this was a year (1850) remarkable for its healthiness. What it would have been in a sickly year, we dare not conjecture.

"We were at first inclined to regard these figures as an exaggeration," adds the above writer. "We could not believe that a portion of Boston is annually almost decimated of its population. But a careful re-examination has confirmed the accuracy of the statement."*

Notwithstanding these evils, the immigrant is generally much better provided for upon his arrival in the United States at the present time than formerly.

" The sufferings attendant on immigration to America are believed to be now much less than they were in the earlier periods of its history. The facilities and safety of navigating the ocean have been vastly increased since the first settlement of the country. This continent and the European have, by the rapidity, frequency and regularity of communication, been comparatively made one country. Now-a-days, the European emigrants, as soon as they arrive at these shores, have stopping places filled with an abundance of the necessaries of life; and when want or sickness befal them, as is often the case, the charitable institutions are opened to soothe their sufferings, and often the hand of individual charity is extended to them in a manner to touch their hearts with emotions of gratitude. But in the time of our fathers, no white man welcomed their coming, no smiling villages cheered their hearts, and, as they advanced to the places of their settlement, they found nothing but a wilderness and wild beasts, and what was often worse than wild beasts—the savages. And now the emigrant, if he plants himself down in the wild lands of America, has the conveniences of an easy transportation, and is furnished at every step of his path with an abundance flowing from a bountiful soil and laid up by an industrious and frugal people. We have not the means at hand of showing distinctly and exactly the comparative distresses; but if the subject were fully inquired into, we have no doubt but that the sufferings and mortality of immigrants to America are now very much less than they were formerly; and we regard this as one of the evidences of improvement in the condition of mankind."†

---

* North Am. Rev., No. CLII., July, 1851, pp. 121-2.   † Chickering's Immigration, p. 53.

What will be the ultimate moral and physical effect of this immense tide of emigration none can determine. Mr. Chickering thus sums up his reasoning concerning it:—

"This migration of masses, numbering of late years more than one hundred thousand annually, now nearly three hundred thousand annually, not in the warlike spirit of the Goths and Vandals who overran the Roman empire, and destroyed the monuments of art, and the evidences of civilization, but in the spirit of peace, anxious to provide for themselves and their children the necessaries of life, and apparently ordained by Providence to relieve the countries of the old world and to serve great purposes of good to mankind,—is one of the most interesting spectacles the world ever saw. This movement is to go on till the western continent is filled with inhabitants. The future destiny of these States none can tell; every accession of new comers introduces new elements of moral and political power into the community, besides the insensible changes which are constantly taking place. If past experience has shown the result of this immigration to America to have been a modification of our institutions and manners from year to year, do not the signs of the times indicate some danger of important changes in the very structure of society, as the current becomes more and more swollen in consequence of the facilitated means of conveyance, and of the multiplied necessities of emigrating."

CHAPTER V.

BIRTHS.

The number of births according to the census returns for 1850, occurring among the white and free colored population for the year preceding the enumeration was 548,837, being 2.75 to every 100 persons, distributed as follows:

States and Territories.	Births.	Ratio per cent.	States and Territories.	Births.	Ratio per cent.
Alabama................	12,265	2.86	New Hampshire......	6,111	1.92
Arkansas...............	5,483	3.36	New Jersey..........	13,556	2.77
California	273	0.29	New York............	76,337	2.46
Columbia, District of....	1,248	2.60	North Carolina.......	16,648	2.87
Connecticut............	7,646	2.06	Ohio.................	56,884	2.87
Delaware...............	2,495	2.80	Pennsylvania	64,331	2.78
Florida.................	1,322	2.75	Rhode Island	3,610	2.45
Georgia................	15,239	2.90	South Carolina.......	6,607	2.33
Illinois.................	26,681	3.13	Tennessee	23,090	3.02
Indiana	32,296	3.27	Texas................	4,765	3.09
Iowa	6,099	3.17	Vermont.............	6,594	2.10
Kentucky	23,805	3.09	Virginia	25,153	2.65
Louisiana	7,292	2.67	Wisconsin	10,424	3.41
Maine	13,995	2.40	Terri- Minnesota ...	168	2.77
Maryland...............	14,036	2.85	tories. New Mexico..	1,233	2.00
Massachusetts..........	23,192	2.33	Oregon......	310	2.33
Michigan	10,898	2.74	Utah........	432	3.80
Mississippi	8,687	2.93			
Missouri..	19,632	3.30	Total	548,837	2.75

This table exhibits a great disparity in the productiveness of the different populations of the various States. While in the Territory of Utah, under the influence of its peculiar institutions, the ratio is 3.80 per cent., in California it dwindles down to the insignificant one of 0.29 per cent.

In this connection, the proportion which the females bear to the males, and the ages of the former, is important. These proportions are here given. For every hundred males there are in the different States, of the ages mentioned, the following number of females:—

States and Territories.	20 and under 30.	30 and under 40.	40 and under 50.	States and Territories.		20 and under 30.	30 and under 40.	40 and under 50.
Alabama	98.2	84.6	85.8	Missouri		85.7	75.0	77.1
Arkansas	87.1	73.8	74.3	New Hampshire		102 5	103.3	103.8
California	3.5	4.5	6.0	New Jersey		102.2	95.5	93.9
Columbia, District of	112.1	97.0	99.1	New York		99.8	91.1	88.9
Connecticut	99.4	96.7	101.6	North Carolina		107.8	108.2	107.9
Delaware	99.7	97.3	94.9	Ohio		94.1	88.8	87.4
Florida	78.0	65.9	67.9	Pennsylvania		98.7	92.3	91.6
Georgia	97.0	90.9	92.4	Rhode Island		103.6	98.6	105.5
Illinois	88.8	79.1	80.5	South Carolina		101.5	98.3	100.2
Indiana	92.5	86.7	90.9	Tennessee		100.7	98.4	101.2
Iowa	93.6	76.7	76.6	Texas		74.8	60.6	62.9
Kentucky	92.5	85.2	88.7	Vermont		93.4	97.4	95.9
Louisiana	79.9	54.8	54.4	Virginia		100.0	97.0	96.2
Maine	93.8	93.5	94.9	Wisconsin		82.5	71.4	72.6
Maryland	95.0	90.5	92.0	Terri- tories.	Minnesota	48.9	34.8	45.1
Massachusetts	106.4	96.5	99.8		New Mexico	99.1	80.8	82.3
Michigan	89.7	81.9	76.2		Oregon	33.7	40.6	47.0
Mississippi	86.9	74.5	77.1		Utah	70.4	78.5	78.7

This table furnishes a very satisfactory solution why a wide difference in births should exist between Utah and California, the proportion of females of an age to adapt them for child-bearing being large in the former, while it is insignificant in the latter. In Utah, there are 101 females between the ages of 15 and 20, 70 between 20 and 30, 78.5 between 30 and 40, and 78.7 between 40 and 50, to every one hundred males; while in California, there are but 19.1 between 15 and 20, 3.5 between 20 and 30, 4.5 between 30 and 40, and 6 between 40 and 50, to each one hundred males.

A comparison of Utah, however, with some other sections of the Union, as the District of Columbia, and the States of Massachusetts, New Hampshire, North Carolina and Tennessee, shows it to possess a considerably less proportional number of females of the ages above indicated than these States. In the District of Columbia, the relative number of females included in these ages is greater than in any other portion of the United States.

The number of births in the parts of the Union above indicated, do not by any manner of means maintain a ratio corresponding to the number of females; those of the District of Columbia being 2.60 per cent.; of Massachusetts, 2.33; of New Hampshire, 1.92; of North Carolina, 2.87; and of Tennessee, 3.02.

The most recently settled Western States appear to be most prolific. Thus, the ratio of births in Arkansas is 3.36 per cent.; in Illinois, 3.13; in Indiana, 3.27; in Iowa, 3.17; in Missouri, 3.30; in Wisconsin, 3.41. This difference is doubtless due to the fact that a larger proportional number of females are joined in wedlock, in the Western than the Eastern States. Unfortunately, the returns do not give the relation of the family to its head, and it is consequently impossible to ascertain, among other important enquiries, the number of those who are living in a single, married, or widowed state, with any degree of certainty. The inference, however, that a larger proportional number of persons are married in the Western than in the Eastern States, is based upon tolerably authentic grounds, and among others upon results of the above table of births.

European authorities, when instituting a comparison into the relative number of births which occur among their own populations, are accustomed to attach great importance to the abundance or scantiness of the crops, and more especially to the wheat crop, as a cause for producing an increased or diminished number of births among a given population. Mr. Milne, in his able work on Annuities, has given a table exhibiting the progress of the population of Sweden and Finland, and the character of the crops from 1749 to 1803, a period of fifty-four years, for the purpose of illustrating this point. The table very clearly establishes that the ratio of births to that of the population, was not uniform, and that those years in which the least number took place, were those which followed a deficient crop.

"It will be observed," remarks Mr. Milne, "that any material reduction in the price of wheat, is almost always accompanied by an increase both of marriages and conceptions, and by a decrease in the number of burials, consequently an increase in the excess of births over the deaths.

"Also, that any material rise in the price is generally attended by a corresponding decrease in the marriages and conceptions, and by an increase in the burials; therefore, by a decrease in the excess of the births above the deaths.

"Thus it appears, that an increase in the quantity of food, or in the facility wherewith the laboring classes can obtain it, accelerates the population, both by augmenting the actual fecundity,* and diminishing the rate of mortality, and that a scarcity of food retards the increase of the people by producing in both ways opposite effects."

With the view of further illustrating this proposition, Mr. Milne constructed a table of the numbers of the marriages, baptisms, and burials in England and Wales, taken from the population returns, with the price of wheat, as given in the Appendix to the Committee of the House of Commons, and certified by the Receiver of Corn Returns.

"This table also shows, that an increase of food increases the actual fecundity, not only by promoting new marriages, but by rendering those already contracted more prolific. Thus:—

There were in the year	Marriages.	Conceptions.	When the price of the quarter of Wheat was
1790	70,648	255,508	£2 13 2
1792	74,919	264,028	2 2 11
Differences..	4,271	8,520	£0 10 3

---

* By the *actual fecundity*, that part only of the absolute physical power of propagation is here to be understood which the actual circumstances allow of being developed."

Whereby it appears that a fall of 10s. 3d. in the price of the quarter of wheat was attended by an increase of 4,271 in the number of the annual marriages, while the annual conceptions were augmented by nearly twice that number. Again—

There were in the year	Marriages.	Conceptions.	When the price of the quarter of Wheat was
1795	68,839	256,781	£3 14 2
1797	74,997	270,535	2 13 1
Differences ..	6,158	13,754	£1 1 1

Where the increase of the conceptions, accompanying the fall of wheat, was more than double that of the marriages.*

The reliability of the facts adduced by Mr. Milne, and the correctness of the reasoning based upon them, when applied to the populous communities of the Old World, do not admit of question. They cannot, however, be applied with equal force to the inhabitants of the New, and especially to that portion embraced within the limits of the United States, because, as it has been already stated, the crops are never so short in any part of the Union as to prove a cause of serious distress to the inhabitants.

But notwithstanding the fact, that there is no portion of the Union where labor is not repaid by a sufficient remuneration to procure an ample supply of food, yet the facility of obtaining this in the newly-settled States, is so much greater than in the older, more especially where they contain populous cities, as to produce a decided impression upon the population which inhabits them.

Even among the humbler classes, who, by their numbers, exercise a preponderating influence over the movements of population, and among

---

* Milne on Annuities, p. 390.

whom adventitious wants may be easily laid aside, the assumption of the burden of a family becomes a subject of much more serious consideration in the older States, where a large part of their earnings must necessarily be expended in their maintenance, than in the new, where the necessaries of life can be obtained upon the most reasonable terms.

A very natural effect of these causes, is to increase the number of marriages in the new States, and to render those already contracted more prolific. This deduction would lead us to anticipate that in any population returns, a larger number of births would be recorded in the new States which are affected by these influences, than in the old, where their effect is either not felt, or if so, in a diminished degree.

It has been asserted that misery tends to the contraction of frequent and reckless marriages, and consequently serves to swell the number of births. Ireland is often cited in illustration of the truth of this position. A recent writer says: "That the ignorance of artificial wants and the destitute condition of the Irish, are strongly conducive to early marriages. As a natural consequence, there is hardly a peasant of twenty who is not married, and invariably the greater the destitution of the people, the greater is the rapidity with which they contract the marriage union."

The Irish census of 1841 includes the number of married, unmarried, and widowed persons of each age; and so far from establishing the facts above enunciated with such apparent confidence, proves that the number of persons above the age of fifteen who are unmarried in Ireland, is greater in proportion than in any country from which returns have been made, thus confirming the position established by Nicander, Wargentin, Messance, and Milne, and other early statisticians, that the increase in the number of births is inseparably associated with a good harvest and a consequently fair supply of food, and that the reverse of these conditions tends to a diminution of their number.

In Ireland, where, even before the taking of the census of 1841, plentiful harvests had for many years been far from frequent, and after proved the exception rather than the rule, a large proportion of unmarried persons might be expected. The annexed tables, taken from the Registrar-General's Report, furnish important data upon this point:—

\multicolumn{5}{c}{Men.}				
Ages.	Unmarried.	Married.	Widowers.	Total.
17–26	633,753	55,407	669	689,829
26–36	235,589	310,492	6,335	552,416
36–46	63,358	324,187	13,914	401,459
46–56	29,176	234,110	22,549	285,835
56	25,864	217,811	68,161	311,836
17 and upwards	987,740	1,142,007	111,628	2,241,375
17–46	932,700	690,086	20,918	1,643,704

\multicolumn{5}{c}{Women.}				
Women aged 15-45.	Estimated numbers in 1841.	Number who bore children in 1842.	Proportion of children registered to 100 women.	Women to one birth nearly
Married.......	1,733,576	489,849	23.3	4
Unmarried	2,078,078	35,294	1.7	59

By this report it appears that of the 689,829 males, between the ages of 17 and 26, but 54,407 were married, and 633,753 were unmarried,—thus disproving in the clearest manner the general allegation, that in this impoverished country the rule is to contract early marriages. Of the entire male population, between the ages of 17 and 46, amounting to 1,643,704, but 690,086 were married.

Among the female portion of the population, between 15 and 45 years, numbering 3,811,654, but 1,733,576, or 45.48 per cent. of those whose age fitted them for procreation, were married.

It would be extremely desirable to ascertain the absolute effect produced by migration from one county to another, and especially from one where the means of obtaining a livelihood were precarious, to another, where they could be readily obtained. It unfortunately happens that here the census returns afford but slight information, and even the registration reports of the several States do not appear to cover this ground.

Nothing is more marked than the change in the habits of the Irish people, in relation to their food upon their arrival in this country. Dr. Wilde, in his " Table of Deaths." which accompanied the census of Ireland, of 1851, states, " that the blight which recently fell upon the potato, produced a deadly famine, because the people had cultivated it so extensively, and were accustomed to its use almost exclusively, and when it failed millions became as utterly destitute as if the island were incapable of producing any other species of sustenance." There are few, in the United States, who do not so far abandon the exclusive use of the potato, to which they were accustomed at home, as to make it an inconsiderable part of their ordinary meals, which usually consist of an intermixture of animal and vegetable food, of which latter the potato, it is true, forms a chief ingredient. Bread is likewise partaken of freely by them, and is as extensively used among the Irish as among the native population.

It is not possible to conceive how a people, who were so much attached to the use of the potato, that a revolution in diet in this respect required " even more than the stern necessity of want before it could be accomplished, or any other description of food made palatable to them," should so suddenly and generally have abandoned their ancient customs and adopted a new diet, when the old one was easily obtained at reasonable rates.

A remarkable feature in the population returns of Ireland, is the large diminution of population which they exhibit between the census of 1841 and that of 1851.

According to the returns of 1841, there were 4,019,576 males, and 4,155,548 females, or 8,175,124 inhabitants. The returns of 1851 show 3,190,506 males, and 3,361,463 females, or 6,551,970 inhabitants, being a decrease of 1,623,154 inhabitants in ten years.

Mr. Thom, in his Statistics of Ireland, thus accounts for this deficiency:

" The emigration of the United Kingdom during the last five years gives an annual average of 284,534 persons. If this emigration be analyzed, the results as regards Ireland will be much more striking. The decrease in the population of Ireland between 1841 and 1851 was 1,623,154. Assuming that nine-tenths of the emigration from Liverpool during those ten years was Irish, and adding thereto the emigration direct from Ireland and in ships chartered by the Land and Emigration Commissioners, we have the following result:—

Nine-tenths of emigration from Liverpool	813,844
Emigration direct from Ireland	441,237
Irish in ships chartered by the Land and Emigration Board	34,052
Total Irish emigration in the 10 years	1,289,133

or more than three-fourths of the whole decrease.

" In regard to the emigration of 1851, the Emigration Officer at Glasgow states that of 14,435 emigrants who sailed from the Clyde to America, about one-third were Irish. Proceeding then in regard to other places on the same estimate, we should assume the Irish emigration of 1851 to have been—

Nine-tenths emigrants from Liverpool	185,414
Emigrants direct from Ireland	62,350
One-third from Glasgow	4,811
Emigrants to Australia in ships chartered by the Land and Emigration Commissioners	4,797
Making a total of	257,372

"By the census return, the population of Ireland, on the 31st March, 1851, amounted to 6,551,970. Assuming that this population were increased by births at the rate of one per cent. per annum, which (taking into account the emigration) was the rate of increase between 1831 and 1841, it would give an annual addition of only 65,157. The emigration, therefore, of 1851, while it nearly doubled the estimated average emigration of the preceding ten years, exceeded any probable increase of the population by nearly 4 to 1. But this calculation, unfavorable as it appears, is clearly below the truth; for the classes that emigrate include a large proportion of the youngest, the healthiest, and most energetic of the adult population, on which the excess of births over deaths mainly depends. We should be disposed to believe that those who remain, including an unusual proportion of the old, the most feeble, and most destitute, do not at the most do more than replace, by births, their losses by deaths. If so, it would follow that the annual decrease of the population in Ireland is not less than the annual amount of the emigration, and that unless the emigration be soon arrested, the country will be deserted by its original population. The Colonial Land and Emigration Commissioners, in their twelfth report, state, that they do not believe that

"'The emigration will be arrested by anything short of a great improvement in the position of the laboring population in Ireland; all those obstacles which in ordinary cases would be opposed to so wholesale an emigration appear in the case of the Irish to be smoothed away. The misery which they have for many years endured has destroyed the attachment to their native soil; the numbers who have already emigrated and prospered remove the apprehension of going to a strange and untried country, while the want of means is remedied by the liberal contributions of their relations and friends who have preceded them. The contributions so made, either in the form of pre-paid passages or of money sent home, and which are almost exclusively provided by the Irish, were returned to us, as in

1848, upwards of	£460,000
1849	540,000
1850	957,000
and 1851	990,000

"'And although it is probable that all the money included in these returns is not expended in emigration, yet as we have reason to know that much is sent home of which these returns show no trace, it seems not unfair to assume that of the money expended in Irish emigration in each of the last four years a very large proportion was provided from the other side of the Atlantic.'"

This large emigration, together with the increased mortality induced by the famine, which reached its culminating point in 1847, affords a satisfactory solution for this remarkable deficiency—a large proportion of what Ireland has thus lost in population, the United States appears to have gained.

The city of Boston has classified the nativities of the parents of the children born within its jurisdiction. From the returns of the City Registrar, for 1855, the following table was compiled:—

Birthplaces of Parents.	Fathers.	Mothers.	Birthplaces of Parents.	Fathers.	Mothers.
Boston	369	430	Scotland	78	59
Massachusetts (out of Boston)	467	408	Ireland	3,019	3,231
Maine	288	330	France	34	23
New Hampshire	251	190	Spain and Portugal	4	4
Vermont	89	62	Germany and Northern Europe	346	273
Connecticut	26	23	British American Provinces	221	252
Rhode Island	13	28	Other Foreign Countries	54	29
Other American States	134	122	Unknown	152	187
England	221	165			
			Totals	5,766	5,766

This table exhibits a very large proportion of births among the foreign population—the greater number of which were of Irish parentage, 3,019 fathers, and 3,231 mothers, or 50.30 per cent. of the whole being emigrants from that country. The census of 1855 makes the entire population of

Boston 162,748 ; which, with the ratio of births, is distributed in Wards, as follows :—

Wards.	Population.	Births.	Ratio.
I.	19,264	764	as 1 to 25.21
II.	15,963	715	" 1 " 22.32
III.	13,175	469	" 1 " 28.09
IV.	7,912	123	" 1 " 64.32
V.	10,428	340	" 1 " 30.67
VI.	11,597	266	" 1 " 43.60
VII.	18,430	750	" 1 " 24.57
VIII.	12,690	434	" 1 " 29.24
IX.	9,541	308	" 1 " 30.97
X.	12,553	445	" 1 " 28.20
XI.	13,264	511	" 1 " 25.96
XII.	17,931	691	" 1 " 25.95
	162,748	5,816	

When compared with the returns of the Irish census, as just noticed, these statistics lead to the irresistible conclusion, that notwithstanding the incidents of bad air, crowded lodgings, and the privations attendant upon emigration among the poor, the physical condition of this people is so altered by emigration, as to render them much more prolific in this country than in their own. A high degree of prosperity however is not always evidenced by a great increase of births, because, among the poor it frequently occurs that excessive mortality among infants, by relieving the mothers of their charge, predisposes to an increase of births. In instituting a comparison, therefore, the rate of mortality among the young as well as the number of births should be taken into consideration.

How much the habits of the Irish population of Boston predisposes to infantile mortality may be gleaned from a knowledge of the localities they inhabit. The largest number of Irish are to be found in Ward No. 8, of the old division. "This section of the city contains the least number of inhabited houses, and at the same time the greatest number of persons to a house, there being an avarage 21.18 individuals to each house. Two houses in the ward contain 19 families each; five houses were occupied by 10 families each; fourteen by 9 families each; thirty-two by 8; and fifty-six by 7 families each."

Most of the apartments thus occupied are illy ventilated, and many are underground or cellar dwellings, where the needy occupants in addition to a depraved air, are subjected to the evils incident to poverty which, under the best circumstances, is accompanied by its train of privations.

From these facts it is reasonable to conclude, that the infantile mortality in this ward is much greater than in those portions of the city where the inhabitants are better provided with airy and wholesome dwellings. As will hereafter be seen, the early mortality of children of foreign parentage greatly exceeds that occurring among those born of native parents, and largely contributes to swell the infantile mortality, which characterizes the mortuary records of the chief towns in the United States.

CHAPTER VI.

RECORD OF BIRTHS IN THE SEVERAL STATES.

The reports of Massachusetts which now contain the results of upwards of fourteen years of registration, furnish very authoritative data, so far as the movements of population in that State are concerned. They reflect high credit upon the State under whose auspices they were produced, and the gentlemen engaged in their elaboration. These reports furnish conclusive evidence of the manner in which the population is affected by a large increase of foreign immigration, and its diffusion among its population. Of all the births and marriages which have occurred since 1849, in Boston, Lowell, Fall River, Lawrence, and perhaps other populous towns, the proportion of the foreign to the native, has been as two of the former to one of the latter.

The ratio of increase has steadily been in favor of the foreign births. The counties most affected in this particular are those within whose limits are centered most of the manufacturing establishments of the State, which are very numerous, and give employment to a large number of workmen. In these establishments, in one capacity or another, employment is obtained by a large number of persons of foreign birth, and hence the influence exercised over the movements of population. In those rural districts where manufacturing establishments do not exist, this influence is not felt. Thus, in the three counties of Barnstable, Dukes and Nantucket, which are essentially agricultural, the foreign population does not exceed ten per cent. of the whole.

The ultimate effect of this extensive immigration upon the future condition of the State, considered in a social or political point of view, however interesting to the political economist, lies beyond the limits of the present enquiry, which is necessarily confined to its effect upon the increase or decrease of population, and the influence it exercises in elevating or depressing its physical standard.

The first registration report of Rhode Island gives the following as the number of births which occurred in the year ending 31st May, 1853. Of American parentage, 874. Foreign, 663. Unknown, 322. Total, 1859. Of which 1810 were white and 49 colored.

The entire population of the State in 1850, was 147,549. A large number of districts failed to make the necessary returns, deducting those which failed from the population, it would leave 96,373 as the portion among whom the 1859 births occurred which have been recorded, being 1 to 51.84 of the inhabitants. The census returns estimate 3,610 as the number of births for 1850, which is a much more probable number than that given by the State authorities.

The second and third Registration Reports of this State are much more exact and reliable than the first. The number of births, according to these returns, in

        1853 was 1793
        1854 " 2105
        1855 " 2926

"We cannot," adds the report, "estimate accurately the proportion of births to population. The city of Providence stands in this respect on a wholly different footing from other places, the city being canvassed for this particular purpose, by inquiries from house to house. The births for 1855 were ascertained in January, 1856. The average monthly number was 133, or nearly twenty in a month more than were reported in previous years. They were one to every thirty of the inhabitants of the city, by the census of 1855.

"In the city of Providence, there were 720 children born in the first six months of the year, and 880 in the last six months. This difference is wholly in the births of children of foreign parentage. 'The children of American parents born were, during the first six months, 319, and during the last six months, 320, showing no difference of any consequence in the seasons; while the children born of foreign parents, were 358 during the first, and 497 during the last six months of the year,—a difference of 139. The children of mixed parentage are omitted.' This difference is ascribed to the depressed condition of public health during a large part of the year 1854, in the summer months of which there was a great increase of mortality, mostly from cholera. This increased mortality was almost confined to the foreign population. 'We have in this fact another illustration of the disastrous effects of an epidemic upon the prosperity of a community, and of the importance of sanitary precautions. An epidemic not only destroys the lives of the people, but also reduces the number of children born.'

"In other parts of the State, there were but sixty more births reported as occurring in the last than in the first six months of the year.

"The parentage of children born is exhibited, in the tables for 1854 and 1855, in a somewhat different manner from that which was adopted previously. The cases of 'mixed' parentage,—where one parent was American, and the other foreign—are distinguished from others. We will show, in a concise form, the births for these two years arranged under three heads,

American, Foreign, and Mixed. Those of unknown parentage are omitted in casting the percentages:—

	American.		Foreign.		Mixed.		Unknown.	Total.	
	No.	Per cent.	No.	Per cent.	No.	Per cent.	No.	No.	Per cent.
Bristol County	238	75.08	57	17.98	22	6.94	65	382	100.00
Kent County	168	70.29	60	25.11	11	4.60	50	289	100.00
Newport County	477	77.56	113	18.37	25	4.07	24	639	100.00
Towns of Prov. Co.	328	62.71	181	34.61	14	2.68	60	583	100.00
Providence City	1266	42.83	1512	51.15	178	6.02	5	2961	100.00
Washington County	132	80.00	29	17.58	4	2.42	12	177	100.00
Whole State	2609	54.18	1952	40.54	254	5.28	216	5031	100.00

"It may be desirable to compare the proportions for the two years together, and also with the results obtained in Massachusetts within a few years past, which will be seen to correspond very closely with our own:—

	Rhode Island.		Massachusetts.
	1854.	1855.	1853–1854.
American	54.71	53.82	54.53
Foreign	40.59	40.50	40.63
Mixed	4.70	5.68	4.84
Total	100.00	100.00	100.00

"The proportion of births of purely foreign parentage in Rhode Island is almost precisely the same in the two years; but there is an increase of about one per cent. in the ratio of mixed parentages. Of these, 124 in the two years were of American fathers and foreign mothers, and 130 were the converse. In the two years taken together, the births of American father and foreign mother, form 2.58 per cent., those of foreign father and American mother form 2.70 per cent. of the whole number.

"As stated in our former report, the births of foreign parentage are in much higher proportion than were the foreign-born population, at the time of the last census. In 1850, the foreign-born inhabitants were not quite one-sixth of all in the State,—16.17 to 100. In the years 1854 and 1855, the children born of foreign parentage were full two-fifths (40.54 to 100) of all those born in the State, whose parentage was reported. This great difference is almost exactly the same as mentioned in our last report. It is probably made up of two elements, the increased proportion of foreign-born inhabitants since 1850, and their being actually more productive for their number. This last circumstance may depend in part on physical and social differences; and in part on the higher proportion of individuals in the early adult age. Such a characteristic may be expected among a class formed by large immigration of persons of both sexes.

"The births of foreign parentage in 1854 and 1855, were in higher ratio than the foreign inhabitants in 1850, in every county; the ratio being more than twice as high in Providence city and Washington county, and more than three times as high in Kent county.

"In the city of Providence, we can compare the births of each class with the population by the census of 1855. In so doing, we will quote from the City Registrar's Report: 'The population of the city, *according to parentage*, by the census of 1855, was, American, 27,897, Foreign, 19,432; but the children born during the same year, if we put those of mixed parentage according to the birth-place of the father, were, American, 685, Foreign, 915, showing an excess of 230 children of foreign parents. Comparing the births with the population, the results are as follows:—

American population.. 58.94 per cent. American children born.. 42.81 per cent.
Foreign population.... 41.06 per cent. Foreign children born.... 57.19 per cent.'

"The births of American parentage in the city were one to 40.7 of the American-born inhabitants; the births of foreign parentage were one in 21.2 of the foreign-born inhabitants. The births of mixed parentage are here classed according to the birth-place of the fathers. It appears, then, that in the city of Providence, the imported population are very nearly twice as productive, for their number, as the native."

The population of Rhode Island is largely engaged in manufacturing, and it is highly probable that the same influences are at work as are developed by the admirable statistics of Massachusetts, in that State. The percentage of foreign to the whole, is nearly 16 per cent., and but little short of that of Massachusetts. Of the entire foreign population of the State, 23,111 in number, 21,434 are from Great Britain and Ireland, 15,944 being from Ireland alone. The larger proportion of these are centered in towns and about the manufacturing establishments.

The registration returns of Connecticut for six years, give the number of births for each year consecutively, as follows:—

1848 6,850	1850 7,578	1853 8,302
1849 7,238	1851 8,362	1854 8,439

The ratio of births to the population in 1850, was one in each forty-five of the inhabitants. The census returns estimate the number of births in 1850 at 7,646, which varies but little from the registration returns. No record is made of the parentage of those who are born, and consequently no comparison can be instituted.

From the returns of New Jersey, it would appear that the number of births in 1854 were less than in 1850—the census returns of that year enumerating 13,556 births, while the registration returns for 1854, give a total of but 12,602 births for that year. The registration report does not include the number of births in the whole State, as thirty-seven townships scattered through the various counties are noted as not making any return whatever, or omitting the number of births. By deducting the population of these townships from that of the whole State, a tolerable approximation to the truth may be obtained.

The registration reports of Kentucky, for 1852 and 1853, which are more reliable than those of any other State, except Massachusetts, show that the number of births in Kentucky in 1852, was 25,906, and in 1853, 26,757. The number returned in 1850, by the census, was 23,805.

The various statistics of births derived from all sources, give an aggregate ratio of one birth to each thirty-five of the inhabitants. That the number has been considerably under-estimated, does not admit of doubt. Many instances of carelessness and omission have already come to light, and how many remain undetected can never, in all probability, be ascertained.

There are reasons why the United States should exhibit a large number of births, instead of the small one indicated by the returns. The argument already adduced, that a plentiful supply of food and fecundity, go hand in hand, should operate with peculiar force, in the case of the population of this country. As its supply of food is superabundant, so should the increase of its population by birth be great. Again, the number of children, under one year of age, in 1850, was 629,446. Now, when the large number of deaths which occur in the first year are taken into consideration, it becomes obvious that a larger proportion of births must have occurred than are represented by the records, in order to admit of the existence of this population.

There are two sources from which a population may derive increase, one by birth, and another by immigration. Allowing the full latitude to the capacity of the latter, which has been assigned to it by Professor Tucker,

Mr. Chickering and others, it still requires a larger increase by births than one in thirty-five, to account for the increase of the population of the whole country, admitting the ratio of deaths to approximate the per centage previously assigned to them.

The annual average births in the principal countries of Europe are detailed in the annexed table:—

	Annual Births to 100 Persons Living.			Persons Living to one Annual Birth.
	Legitimate.	Illegitimate.	Both.	
France	2,632	.205	2,837	35
England	2,992	.216	3,208	31
Prussia	3,507	.260	3,767	27
Austria	3,452	.422	3,874	26
Russia	.....	...	4,284	23

While the number in England reaches 1 in 31, in Prussia 1 in 27, in Austria 1 in 26, and in Russia 1 in 23, there appears to exist no cause why in the United States, where the increase in population is so much greater than any of these countries, the number of births should be but 1 in 35.

Now all those who were under one year of age, at the taking of the census in 1850, must have been born within the twelve months preceding. If to the 629,446 persons below the age of one year there enumerated, be added twenty per cent. for loss by deaths, which corresponds tolerably well with the Massachusetts returns, the number born in that year would have been 755,336, or one to each thirty inhabitants, a number nearly corresponding to that of England, and much more in accordance with the ratio of increase of population than the estimate of births heretofore given.

It is rendered obvious, by a comparison of the relative proportion of births in different parts of the country, that the same causes which have been found to exercise an influence in the increase or diminution of their numbers in other countries, operate with equal force in this, and if the causes to which reference has been made be found to produce results in obedience to acknowledged laws, when applied to a comparison of one section with another, there is no reason for not admitting their application, when making a comparison of the country with other countries as a whole.

With the view of ascertaining the natural increase of the whole population by birth, Professor Tucker instituted a comparison between the white females in the several States, as returned by each census, and the number of children under ten years of age.

An examination of the percentage of births is given by Professor Tucker, while it clearly demonstrates a gradual falling off of the whole number, as compared with the existing population, at the same time shows a much greater number than one birth to each thirty-five inhabitants, after making a proper deduction for loss by deaths in the early periods of life. These results, so far from exciting surprise, are precisely what might have been anticipated in a new country whose increase of population has been rapid, and a considerable portion of whose territory has within the memory of those now living been converted from a wilderness into well peopled districts, covered with cultivated fields, and considerable towns. In the earlier period of these settlements experience demonstrates that the number of married persons is more numerous, and the proportion of births greater, than at a later period, when questions of prudence operate in retarding marriage, and diminishing the relative number of births.

CHAPTER VII.

PROPORTION OF THE SEXES AT BIRTH.

The proportion of the sexes at birth would appear to be regulated by some general law, which operates with tolerable uniformity in giving a slight preponderance to the male over the female births. Although this proportion is nearly the same in all countries and at remote periods of time, yet it is liable to a slight variation, which manifests itself in every return of births, so that it rarely happens that two returns exhibit the same relative number of male and female births.

The reason for the want of uniformity in returns apparently collected under like circumstances, and yet which approach so nearly as to produce an admirable equipoise among the sexes, is among the questions for which no satisfactory solution has been offered.

Dr. Curtis, in the eighth registration report of Massachusetts, has given a table comprising the number of births which occurred in that commonwealth, for the five years intervening between January 1st, 1845, and January 1st, 1850, with the months in which they took place, and the number of male and female births. This table, which embraces 92,272 births, is appended :—

Months.	Whole Number.	Sex.			Proportion.		Females in each 10,000 Males.
		Males.	Females.	Unknown.	Males.	Females.	
January	7478	3833	3572	73	51.76	48.24	9319
February	7533	3817	3640	76	51.18	48.82	9558
March	8352	4283	3977	92	51.85	48.15	9286
April	7920	4030	3771	119	51.66	48.34	9357
May	6804	3552	3194	58	52.66	47.34	8989
June	6934	3565	3306	63	51.81	48.19	9301
July	7804	3918	3833	53	50.22	49.78	9910
August	8267	4225	3992	50	51.44	48.56	9440
September	8251	4136	4053	62	52.18	47.82	9164
October	7974	4115	3791	68	52.06	47.94	9208
November	7446	3899	3499	48	52.70	47.30	8975
December	7509	3855	3586	68	51.81	48.19	9301
Total	92,272	47,228	44,214	830	51.65	48.35	9362

In the fourteenth registration report of Massachusetts, Dr. Shurtleff has given a table containing the births for five years, ending with 1855, which is also appended:—

Sex.	1850.	1851.	1852.	1853.	1854.	1855.	Aggregate.	Per Centage.
Males	14,137	14,949	15,246	15,798	16,352	16,785	93,267	51.33
Females	13,392	13,613	14,432	14,965	15,469	15,888	87,759	48.16
Unknown	135	119	124	157	176	172	883	.51
Totals	27,664	28,681	29,802	30,920	31,997	32,845	181,909	100.00

The construction of these tables is different, and intended to answer different questions, yet they both reply to the one which is propounded to them as to the relative proportion of the sexes at birth.

Together they embrace the record of 274,181 births, and extend over a period of eleven years. It will be seen, that in obedience to the law already spoken of, the number of male births is invariably in the preponderance, and in correspondence with the law of variation, the relative proportion of the two sexes is never in any two returns alike. Of the 92,272 births included in Dr. Curtis's table, 47,228 were males, and 44,214 females. This gives the relative proportion of 107 males to 100 females, but during the last two years the males bore the proportion of 108 to 100 females. In the year 1850, the excess of male births was 745; in 1851, 1,336; in 1852, 814; in 1853, 833; in 1854, 883; and in 1855, 897. Thus the relative proportion of the sexes within certain limits is ever varying—the year 1849, which had an excess of 1,066 male births was succeeded by a year in which they had declined to 745, and this again was succeeded by one in which they had risen to 1,336.

Dr. Curtis separated the births which occurred in town in the year 1849, from those which took place in rural districts, with the following result:—

	City.	Country.
Males	5,344	7,985
Females	5,106	7,167
Unknown	16	155
Total	10,466	15,307
Proportion of Females in each 10,000 Males	9,555	8,976

This table shows, that while the percentage of male births in the country was 52.70, it had declined in town to 51.14, or 1.56 per cent. less than in the country. The division denominated "city," contained nine cities and three towns, having over 10,000 inhabitants each.

The 1859 births, which are noted in the registration returns of Rhode Island, for the year 1853, are divided into 942 males, 899 females, and 18 unknown, being in the ratio of 104 males to 100 females. It may be noted as a curious circumstance, that of the thirty-nine births occurring in Providence county among the colored inhabitants, but seventeen were males, and twenty-two were females. The preponderance of all the births in the county, however, was in favor of the males.

Of those which took place in 1854, 1081 were males, 1003 females, and 21 are unknown; and of those which occurred in 1855, 1492 were males, 1421 females, and 13 of unknown sex.

"The number of males born," adds the report, "in all our returns, exceeds that of females, in the proportion of a little more than four and four-tenths per cent.* An excess of male over female births is generally found in prosperous communities. It is a remarkable fact, one which we may be happy that the information now before us gives us no means of illustrating, that periods of general calamity are followed by a lessened preponderance in the number of male births, or even an excess of females. Thus it has been observed that children born nearly a year after the prevalence of epidemic cholera, in Philadelphia and also in Paris, twenty-five years ago, show a preponderance of female births. On the other hand, the favorable circumstances of plentiful food, pure air, wholesome and sufficient occupation, without overworking,—all have been found to increase the proportion of male births. In this point of view, our returns are not very favorable indications of the state of our people. In Massachusetts, for the five years, 1849–1853, the excess of male births was about seven per cent. In Philadelphia, according to Dr. Gouverneur Emerson, who has directed particular attention to this point, it is about 7 per cent.; in England, about 5; in France and Prussia, about 7; while 'in the rural districts of the United States, and especially in the newest settlements,' it is supposed to be not less than 10 per cent. We trust that fuller returns will enable this State to make a more favorable show; and we note this comparison, not to throw a slur on the manly force of our State, but to provoke, if possible, more exact attention hereafter to this inquiry, which is considered one of the tests by which the welfare of a community may be judged.†

---

* That is, for every 1000 females, about 1044 males were born.
† 2d Registration Report Rhode Island, p. 16.

The number of births in the City of Providence for 1856 was 1675, of which 891 were males, and 784 females. The proportion was one birth to 29.3 inhabitants.

"The proportion of the sexes shows a remarkable increase in the relative number of males, being 53.19 males and 46.81 females in each 100 children born, or 113.6 males to 100 females. In the State of Massachusetts, during six years from 1849–54 inclusive, the proportion was 51.37 males, and 48.12 females in each 100 children born, and in the State of Rhode Island for the year 1855, the proportions were, males 51.22 per cent., females 48.78 per cent., or 105 males to 100 females.

"Bearing in mind the proposition stated in last year's report, that 'the proportion of the sexes at birth depends upon the location, occupation, and sanitary condition of a community, the proportion of males being greatest where all circumstances are most favorable to health and prosperity,' the proportions for the year 1856, would indicate an unusually healthy condition of the city.

"The proportion of the sexes born in Providence during two years was:

"In 1855, males 50.44 per cent.; females 49.56 per cent.
In 1856, males 53.19 per cent.; females 46.81 per cent."*

The table of births for the State of New Jersey, already given, divides the sexes into 6,153 males, 5,646 females, and 803 not designated, or 108 male to 100 female births.

The number of births returned under the registration system of Virginia for 1853, was 31,518, divided as follows:

Males,	16,180
Females,	14,160
Unknown,	1,178
Total,	31,518

---

* 2d Report of E. M. Snow, M. D., Registrar of Providence.

Or in the proportion of 114 males to 100 female births. The returns embrace the births in 114 out of 137 counties, leaving 23 counties from which returns were not received. The births embraced in the census report for 1850, were 25,153. A comparison with this return renders it probable that the number of births returned by the 114 counties in 1853 is tolerably accurate.

From the returns of Kentucky the following table is deducted:—

Births in	1852.	1853.	Males to 100 Females.
Males,	13,625	13,027	112
Females,	12,109	11,805	110
Unknown,	172	173	
Total,	25,906	25,005	

A very remarkable feature connected with the returns of births in Virginia and Kentucky is the large preponderance of male over female births. It unfortunately happens that no returns are made by other neighboring States by which to institute a comparison. There are some reasons for placing reliance upon the accuracy of these returns so far as they have been rendered. The inhabitants of both of these States are, for the most part, engaged in agricultural pursuits, the number of manufactures and populous towns being comparatively small, and the residents of the country greatly preponderating over those of towns. Agriculture in these States, as indeed in all southern States, is considered a dignified occupation, while commerce and the mechanic arts are deemed ignoble. The direct effect of this state of things is to entice into the pursuit of agriculture the most intelligent and cultivated class of the community and to leave in town those who are least so.

There is consequently scattered over every portion of Virginia and Kentucky an agricultural population of high intelligence, who are the patrons of the humbler classes surrounding them, and take great interest in the most minute details of their daily concerns. An individual engaged in collecting statistical information among such a population as has been described, would find no difficulty in obtaining the facts from those whose opinions were entitled to confidence.

From this it would appear extremely probable, that the sex in the cases of reported births, was correctly ascertained. But the wide disparity in the proportion of the sexes at birth, observed in Kentucky in the two years of registration, being no less than two per cent., together with the great difference, existing between this State and Virginia, as compared with the more northern States, where births have been recorded, as indeed with the observations of the European States, would lead to the belief that some error existed which time and careful scrutiny may hereafter develope.

The city of Charleston, in South Carolina, while taking a census in 1848, obtained by the personal enquiries of its agents the number of births which had occurred in the year for which the census was taken, the results of which are as follows:—

Wards.	WHITES.			SLAVES.			FREE COLORED.		
	Males.	Females.	Totals.	Males.	Females.	Totals.	Males.	Females.	Totals.
1	40	30	70	44	44	88	4	2	6
2	45	49	94	78	61	139	10	7	17
3	70	76	146	50	45	95	4	7	11
4	74	81	155	86	76	162	13	9	22
Total....	229	236	465	258	226	484	31	25	56

As the facts here exhibited are somewhat curious, it has been deemed advisable to allow the report from which they are taken to explain them for itself. It may be proper to remark, that the census report and accompanying tables were prepared by Dr. J. L. Dawson, who has for many years held the post of City Register, and as such has prepared the yearly bills of mortality, and Dr. H. W. De Saussure, editor of the Southern Journal of Medicine and Pharmacy.

"The proportion which the male bear to the female births, in each class of the population, appears from the following table :—

WHITES.

	Births.	Proportion.	
Male,	229	49.24=97.00	: or 100.
Female,	236	50.76 100.	to 103.00
	465	100.00	

SLAVES.

	Births.	Proportion.	
Male,	258	53.31=100.00	: or 112.03
Female,	226	46.69 87.58	to 100.
	484	1000.00	

FREE COLORED.

	Births.	Proportion.	
Male,	31	55.36=100.	: or 124.01
Female,	25	44.64 80.63	to 100.
	56	100.00	

"It appears that during the year 1848, the male births among the white population were less by 3 per cent. than the female. This must be considered an exceptional year in this respect, for in almost all years in which enumerations of the population have been made, the males have exceeded the females, and a reference to the subject of 'public health' will show that the male deaths exceed the female. As there are no other years, however, with which the births can be compared, the present proportions

MALE AND FEMALE POPULATION.

must remain, to be corrected by future observations. Among the slave and free colored population, the male exceed the female births by 13, and 20 per cent.; there must, however, be a greater mortality of males in these classes at the early ages than of the females—for at 10 years the females exceed the males among the slaves, and the female free colored exceed the males at all ages."*

With the exception of the births of the white population of Charleston, which may be looked upon as an anomaly, and not in conformity with the laws which regulate the proportion of the sexes in that city even, all the records adduced show a preponderence of male over female births sufficient, notwithstanding the higher rate of mortality prevailing among the male sex, to give them a slight advantage in numbers in each section of the country except the New England States, where the female population is in excess, as will be seen by the following table:—

Geographical Divisions.	Males.	Females.	Proportion of females to 100 males.
New England,	1,346,680	1,358,415	100.87
Middle States,	3,186,102	3,112,945	97.70
Southern States,	1,154,010	1,137,156	98.54
South-Western States	1,069,991	980,791	91.66
North-Western,	3,135,333	2,888,030	92.11
Territories and California,	134,286	49,329	36.73

Whether the ratio of increase and mortality, with slight variations, is uniformly the same under all varieties of climate, temperature, and individual relations, or whether the male sex is exposed under some circumstances to a higher rate of mortality than the female, and the equality is maintained by an increased relative number of male births, are questions which the statistics of the United States at present collected, do not afford a solution for. Those of the different countries of Europe, although extend-

---

* Census of Charleston, page 181.

ing over a greater length of time, and possessing more exactness, are necessarily limited as to their range of climate, and could not answer this enquiry as satisfactorily as those of the United States, if they were equally extensive and reliable.

But whether the laws which regulate the relative proportion of the sexes at birth, in old and new countries, in hot and temperate latitudes, in town and country, be diverse or the same, as an element of information and a matter for curious speculation it furnishes one of the most important enquiries connected with births, and is absolutely indispensable to a just estimate of population.

"Taking the average of the whole of Europe," says Dr. Carpenter, "the proportion is about 106 males to 100 females. It is curious, however, that this proportion is considerably different for legitimate and illegitimate births, the average of the latter being 102½ to 100, in places where the former was 105¾ to 100. This is probably to be accounted for by the fact, which is one of the most remarkable contributions that has yet been made by statistics to physiology, that the sex of the offspring is influenced by the relative ages of the parents. The following table expresses the average results obtained by M. Hofacker, in Germany, and by Mr. Sadler, in Britain, between which it will be seen there is a manifest correspondence, although both were drawn from too limited a series of observations. The numbers indicate the proportion of male births to 100 females under the several conditions mentioned in the first column:

	Hofacker.		Sadler.
Father younger than mother,	90.6	Father younger than mother,	86.5
Father and mother of equal age,	90.0	Father and mother of equal age,	94.8
Father older by 1 to 6 years,	103.4	Father older by 1 to 6 years,	103.7
" " " 6 to 9 "	124.7	" " " 6 to 11 "	126.7
" " " 9 to 18 "	143.7	" " " 11 to 16 "	147.7
" " " 18 and more,	200.0	" " " 16 and more,	163.2

From this it appears, that the more advanced age of the male parent has a very decided influence in occasioning a preponderance in the numbers of male infants, and as the state of society generally involves a condition of this kind in regard to marriages, whilst in the case of illegitimate children the same does not hold good, the difference in the proportional number of male births is accounted for. We are not likely to obtain data equally satisfactory in regard to the influence of more advanced age on the part of the female parent as a difference of 10 or 15 years on that side is not so common. If it existed to the same extent, it is probable that the same law would he found to prevail in regard to female children born under such circumstances as has been stated with regard to the male;—namely, that the mortality is greater during embryonic life and early infancy, so that the preponderance is reduced."*

A question akin to the one just discussed, and indeed necessarily linked with it is, that of the proportion of still-born to those who survive and the relative proportion of the sexes among them. In regard to both the absolute number of still-born and their relative division into sexes the returns are exceedingly incomplete. The State of Massachusetts is now enabled to furnish the most complete records, but even among the ordinarily exact statistics of that State, in a very large proportion of cases, the sex of the still-born child has been overlooked.

During the five years, 1849-53, in which 142,830 living births are recorded, there occurred 2,618 still-born cases, of which 827 were males and 574 females, and 1,217 where sex is not designated:—

Born Alive.	Still-born.	Proportion of Still-born to each 10,000.
142,830	2,618	180

" It has been a subject of complaint in nearly every report, that suffi-

---

* Carpenter's Physiology, p. 1014.

cient pains have not been taken in ascertaining the sex and other particulars relating to stillborn children. A very little labor would ensure more accurate returns than are now had on this particular, which is of considerably more importance in vital and mortuary statistics than is generally attributed to it by those who have little or no interest in investigations of this sort. As far as results have been obtained that can be relied upon, it is very certain that the prevailing sex in this Commonwealth has been males. It is hoped that future abstracts will show that more regard is beginning to be felt on this subject of statistical inquiry."*

The returns from Virginia show the following results:—

Born Alive.	Still-born.	Proportion of Still-born to each 10,000.
31,518	836	268

The registration report of Kentucky for 1852, contains, in round numbers, 800 cases of still-born children. The report, in alluding to this portion of the return remarks, that the still-born certainly appear to be in large proportion—no less than 3.09 per cent. of all the births. This may be so, yet there is reason to believe that it is too large, because a number of children are returned as still-born who have names. There is reason to believe that a number of assessors mistook the precise import of the terms "alive" and "dead," and returned as dead those which were dead at the time of making the assessment.†

The number of still-born returned for 1853, is 633; of which 467 were whites and 166 colored:—

	Born Alive.	Still-born.	Proportion of Still-born to each 10,000.
Whites,	19,796	467	228
Colored,	5,209	166	313
Total	25,005	633	252

---

* 14th Registration Report for Massachusetts, p. 192.
† Registrar Report for Kentucky for 1852, page 105.

SEX OF STILL-BORN.

	Males.	Females.	Unknown.	Total.
White,	270	191	6	467
Colored,	90	72	4	166
Total,	360	263	10	633

For the purpose of enabling a comparison to be instituted between the relative proportion of still-born to the living births in this country and Europe, the following tables have been introduced.

ABSTRACT OF THE BIRTHS IN PRUSSIA, FRANCE, SAXONY AND BELGIUM.

	Births.	Still-born.
Prussia (1820–34)—Males,	3,906,544	147,705
Females,	3,686,473	109,363
Total,	7,593,017	257,063
* France (1842.)—Males,	506,309	17,969
Females,	476,587	12,397
Total,	982,896	30,366
† Austria (1834–7–9.)—Males,	1,259,372	
Females,	1,189,627	
Total,	2,448,999	30,147
‡ Saxony (1832–41.)—Males,	338,239	17,618
Females,	317,102	12,839
Total,	655,341	30,457
§ Belgium (1842.)—Males,	70,676	3,196
Females,	67,459	2,336
Total,	138,135	5,532

* M. Moréau de Jounés. † Beecher, pp. 259–261. ‡ Hoffman. § Census.

The annexed table from an excellent article on Infantile Mortality, by Dr. Tripe, shows the percentage of males and females among the still-born in the countries mentioned :—

	Males.	Females.	Percentage.	
			Males.	Females.
France (three years)	67,356	46,637	100.0	69.2
Austria (four years)	25,288	17,351	100.0	68.6
Belgium	38,312	28,359	100.0	74.0
Saxony (ten years)	17,618	12.839	100.0	72.9
Prussia (three years)	24,838	19,036	100.0	76.6

"The results of this table," adds Dr. Tripe, "are very striking, for we see that to each 1000 males who are still-born, there are in France only 692, in Austria 686, in Prussia 766, in Belgium 740, and in Saxony 729, still-born females. The variations in the ratios are by no means great, and they are yet smaller in each country during a period of years than those shown in the above table for different countries. This cannot be proved here, for want of space. It will be noticed that the variation does not amount to five and a half per cent., although the statistics are collected from such different nations and races; showing that the law is general, and that the cause of the excess of male deaths over those of females commences at the earliest period of life, and diminishes, as we have already shown, as age advances, even from the first month, and most probably week, of extra uterine life.

"This opinion receives very strong confirmation by a comparison of the ratios of still-born male and female children with those of children who die during the first month. We find in Belgium that the proportion of still-born female children to that of males is 740 to 1000; whilst that of deaths under one month old is 749 to 1000; and in England (years 1839–44) 765 to 1000."*

---

* Brit. and Foreign Med-Chi. Review for April, 1857, p. 348.

Among the earliest records of the proportion of still-born to those born alive, are those given by Mr. Wargentin, in 1776, of the births in Sweden and Finland, for nine years, ending in 1763. During these nine years there were—

	Born alive.	Still-born.	Proportion of still-born to each 10,000.
Males,	44,954	1269	282
Females,	43,078	963	217
	88,032	2205	250

These results are interesting as a standard of comparison, because they were made at a period of time comparatively remote from the present, and during the interval which has elapsed many changes are supposed to have been introduced into the practice of obstetrics, by means of which labor is facilitated, and the life of the fœtus placed in less jeopardy. Yet a comparison of the returns in both countries shows about the same results, and certainly does not furnish as strong an argument in favor of the advance of obstetrical skill as might naturally have been anticipated. In this respect, the returns from Virginia and Kentucky are less favorable than those from Massachusetts; for while the former assimilate very nearly to those derived from Sweden, by Wargentin, the latter exhibit a decided diminution in the number of still-born. The inference is that the Massachusetts returns are more complete in this respect, than those of Virginia and Kentucky.

It has been observed that in every return the number of still-born males was greater than that of the females. Dr. Clark, the physican to the Dublin Lying-in Hospital, contributed a paper to the Royal Society, which appeared in the seventy-sixth volume of the Philosophical Transactions, assigning as a chief cause for the greater number of male than female deaths, the increased size of the male fœtus, which not only requires more sustenance before birth, than the female, but has greater difficulties to encounter in the process of parturition. Whenever therefore any delicacy of constitution on the part of the mother, prevents her from yielding to the fœtus in utero a proper amount of nutriment, or a physical malformation presents an obstacle at the moment of birth, the chances of death are largely increased in the male child over those of the female.

These observations are undoubtedly correct, and have received the confirmation of subsequent writers. An additional cause assigned by Dr. Clark in the same paper, although supported by some plausible reasons, does not appear to be quite so clear. This is that the greater size of the male child renders it more liable to the inherited infirmities of the father, as well as to the results of the defective constitution of the mother.

CHAPTER VIII.

THE EFFECT OF SEASONS ON CONCEPTION.

The effect of the seasons in influencing conception, is as elsewhere quite manifest in the returns of births in the United States.

The table for five years, prepared by Dr. Curtis, from the Registration Reports of Massachusetts, (page 68,) shows that the largest number of births occurred in March, and that the next months most prolific in births were August and September. From this isolated example, the inference might be drawn that June was the month most favorable to conception, and that November and December were the next most favorable months, these being the months in which the conceptions took place which produced the births in March, August and September. The least number of births occurred in May and June, from which it might be inferred that August and September were the least prolific months in the year.

Dr. W. L. Sutton, of Georgetown, Kentucky, has prepared a table, from the births occurring in that State in 1853, to illustrate this point, which is annexed:—

Date of Conception.	Male.	Female.
March,	M 1,431	M 1,302
February,	1,162	1,038
January,	1,111	1,035

Date of Conception.	Male.	Female.
November,	1,128	984
December,	1,133	966
June,	1,106	897
July,	1,024	906
August,	946	972
May,	960	896
October,	987	863
September,	919	886
April,	m 909	m 842*

From this table it would appear the month of March was by far the most prolific, and that February and January followed next in succession; while October, September, and April appear to be the least prolific.

The wide difference in the proportion of births in the different months of the year observable in this table, is somewhat remarkable, and would appear to indicate that the returns upon which it is based are far from complete.

By a comparison of the results of these tables, it will be seen that the prolific months in that prepared by Dr. Curtis are not the same as in that arranged by Dr. Sutton. Upon this point there appears to be no correspondence, and it would seem that the most reasonable inference to be drawn from the facts as thus enunciated, is that if fecundity is influenced by particular seasons, and in this respect is amenable to fixed laws, then the laws which so regulate it are not the same in the States of Massachusetts and Kentucky.

Mr. Milne, for the purpose of determining this question, arranged two tables, one for Sweden and Finland, based upon the observations of Mr. Nicander, which gives the annual averages of conceptions for twenty years, terminating with 1795; the other for Montpellier, in the South of France,

---

* M indicates Maximum, and m minimum, in all these tables.

upon data procured from the Memoir of M. Morgue, which gives the averages of conceptions for twenty-one years, terminating with 1792.

A table formed of these is introduced, in order that a comparison may be made between them and those of Drs. Curtis and Sutton. The comparison is valuable, not only because of the space of time which has elapsed between the making of the observations, but also because they were made in countries bearing a parallel to each other in point of geographical position; thus Sweden may be said to possess a climate somewhat similar to Massachusetts, while Montpellier and Kentucky correspond with each other in this respect :—

TABLE SHOWING THE INTENSITY OF FECUNDITY IN EACH MONTH.						
In Sweden and Finland.				In Montpellier, France.		
Marriages.	Conceptions.		Month.	Conceptions.		Marriages.
	Male.	Female.		Female.	Male.	
1519	4276	4106	January,	1044	1156	596
1385	4210	4020	Febry.	M 1185	M 1221	M 1155
1369	4287	4066	March,	1067	1173	159
1792	4452	4277	April,	1145	1210	403
1393	4377	4213	May,	1090	1183	526
1957	4525	4376	June,	989	1056	472
1071	4342	4163	July,	916	918	447
m 732	3889	3763	August,	m 863	934	434
1539	3696	3547	Sept.	866	m 909	523
M 4267	m 3632	m 3508	October,	940	993	444
3251	3927	3726	Nov.	1007	1086	625
3798	M 4708	M 4485	Dec.	1033	1080	m 142
24,073	50,321	48,250	Total,	12,145	12,919	5,926

Proportion of those born alive to the still-born in Sweden:—

Males, } as 10,000 { 310
Females, }   to   { 238
Total, }   { 275

Still-born males to still-born females, average 13,558 to 10,000

Upon an examination of the Swedish table, it will be seen that in the month of December the greatest number of conceptions took place, while the fewest occurred in September and October. The Montpellier table, on the contrary, exhibits the largest number in February, and the smallest in August and September. Now, there does not appear to be any more correspondence, in the maximum periods of conception, between Sweden and the South of France, than there is between Massachusetts and Kentucky; but if a comparison be made between Sweden and Massachusetts, and a similar one between Montpellier and Kentucky, it will be seen that in both instances there is a remarkable identity between them. In Sweden and Massachusetts the month most favorable to conception is December, while in Kentucky the largest number occurred in March, and in Montpellier in February.

The isolated facts connected with the births of Kentucky for a single year, and those of Massachusetts for five years, do not furnish sufficient grounds upon which to found a conclusion as important as this, yet when taken in connection with other circumstances attendant upon the movements of population, it seems difficult to resist the conclusion, that in different latitudes there are different laws affecting the human species, beginning with conception and terminating with the last moment of existence.

Mr. Milne, whose opinions are usually adopted with great caution, and are entitled to the highest respect, sees, in the tables he adduces, decided evidence of the influence of the seasons upon conceptions, and concludes that if it were not for the disturbing element of marriage, which is not so accurately regulated as that of births, this influence would be still more manifest.

"The rate of frequency of the conceptions in Sweden does in fact come twice in the year to a maximum, and twice to a minimum. Taking the totals for an example, it will be found that having been at a maximum in December, they begin the year by decreasing, and continues to fall till February, when they attain their first minmum ; then rise till June, when they are at their first maximum from that time they continue to fall till October, when they are at the minimum of the whole year, and from thence they rise till December, when they attain to the maximum of the year."*

If the table of Massachusetts were substituted for that of Sweden, and analyzed by the above quotation from Milne, it would be found to correspond in all its parts, and to present a parallelism too exact in detail to be otherwise than the result of a fixed law, which operates at the present day upon a population far removed from the scene of the original observations, and which had scarcely an existence at the time they were made, as it did in the last century upon the inhabitants of Sweden.

And although the correspondence in detail between Montpellier and Kentucky is not as exact as that between Sweden and Massachusetts, yet it is sufficiently so to seem to indicate the direction of a general principle, and it is more than probable that when the returns of Kentucky shall have attained the exactness which characterizes those of Montpellier, and cover a sufficient space of time to give them authority, they will develope with greater exactness the operations of this law.

The opinion is entertained by Mr. Milne, that if it were not for the derangement produced in the movements of conception by marriage, that the maximum would occur about midsummer instead of the winter months, as shown by the European tables above inserted.

---

* Milne on Annuities, p. 503.

CHAPTER IX.

MARRIAGES.

The number of marriages to that of births is about one of the former to four of the latter, yet notwithstanding their small number, the irregularity of their distribution is supposed to exert such an influence over the natural order of births as to disturb, in the manner heretofore indicated, the effect of the different periods of the year upon them. The Swedish and Montpellier tables are accompanied by a column giving the number of marriages which took place in each month, based upon the same elements of calculation as the columns of births, for the purpose of illustrating their effect upon births.

Subjoined will be found a table of the marriages which occurred in Massachusetts for twelve years, ending 31st December, 1855, so arranged as to indicate the number in each month, and a comparison of the whole with the last year. The number of marriages thus tabulated amount to 105,700. This number although small when placed in comparison with those embraced in many of the tables of the older countries of Europe, and indeed with that of the Swedish tables already introduced, exhibits with tolerable certainty, the habits of the population in this regard upon whom the selection of time mainly depends.

Months.	1855.	12 Years.	Average.	Months.	1855.	12 Years.	Average.
January	1,131	9,311	776	September	1,038	9,057	754
February	1,001	7,088	591	October	1,229	10,824	903
March	m658	m5,806	m484	November	M1 516	M13,984	M1,166
April	1,079	8,829	736	December	893	8,313	693
May	1,118	9,645	804	Unknown	46	605	50
June	900	8,152	679				
July	896	7,160	596				
August	824	6,906	576	Totals	12,329	105,700	8,808

While this table exhibits great similarity of results so far as particular months are concerned, yet it shows a great disproportion in the number of marriages in the different months. The largest number took place uniformily, throughout the whole period of twelve years, in the month of November, while the least occurred in March.

The following table, showing the number of marriages which took place in Kentucky, in 1852 and 1853, and the months in which they were solemnized, indicates December as the maximum, and July as the minimum months:—

	1852.	1853.
January,	348	346
February,	357	365
March,	398	435
April,	326	304
May,	272	316
June,	300	294
July,	283	276
August,	390	435
September,	521	499
October,	581	604
November,	558	515
December,	755	656
Unknown,	16	116
Total,	5,105	5,161

The preference for particular months would appear to indicate that some peculiarity in the habits and customs of the inhabitants of the different States lay at the foundation. Mr. L. Shattuck assigns as a reason, that November is the month in which occurs the New England festival of Thanksgiving, when family circles meet together and are presented to their newly-formed marriage connexions.

This period of festivity, so universally observed by the inhabitants of New England, is almost entirely disregarded by the residents of the Southern States. Dr. Sutton supposes that the festivities of Christmas may induce the more frequent selection of December, in Kentucky. It is quite certain, that in the two States whose marriage returns are here given, the festive period takes place in different months, and this difference is manifest in the number of marriages which occur in each, at the season which is celebrated with most glee by its inhabitants.

The large number of marriages among foreigners, included in the Massachusetts returns, could not have been influenced by this custom, which is purely local, and derives its origin from the early Puritan settlers of New England. An examination of the returns in detail, for each registration year, shows that the marriages among the foreign residents are not largely in excess at this period, as are those among the natives of New England, which would seem to corroborate the correctness of the cause assigned by Mr. Shattuck, more particularly as similar causes are supposed to produce like results in other countries.

Mr. Wargentin remarks, that there are always many more marriages contracted during the autumn and winter in Sweden, than in the spring and summer, because the harvest produces abundance, and the cattle are killed in autumn, so that the bulk of the people, who are neither sufficiently rich, nor economical to maintain an equable expenditure, are then best able to give the entertainments that are customary on such occasions.*

"And M. Mourgue informs us that at Montpellier, the month of February always furnishes the greatest number of marriages at the epoch *la fin du Carnaval*, and next to that the month of November, before the epoch called *les Avents*."† The seasons which succeed both of these epochs are those of fasting, in which the Catholic Church, the prevalent one at Montpellier, discountenances as far as possible the solemnization of the rite of matrimony. Besides, the end of Carnival is a period of more boisterous hilarity than the Thanksgiving of New England or the Christmas holiday rejoicings of the Southern States.

The ages of the persons who contract marriage relations, furnishes a very important element in all questions tending to elucidate the influence which this compact has upon society. Upon this subject the Registrar General of England, with great propriety remarks, that "it is not a little remarkable, that although the increase of population and the influence of early and late marriages on the welfare of nations, have for the whole of the present century occupied public attention, and been made the basis of theories which have guided or based legislation, no provision has yet been made for determining the simplest fundamental facts—the foundation of all reasoning on the subject—such as the age of mothers, of children, and the numbers of married and single persons at the several periods of life. Upon many of these points the greatest ignorance prevails, writers on population depending on rough approximations, derived from scanty, imperfect and erroneous data, because the censuses and registers have not yet been taken and abstracted upon a comprehensive and well considered plan."

These observations, which had exclusive reference to the English

---

* Memoires abrégés de l'Academie de Stockholm, p. 32.
† Milne on Annuities, p. 501.

system of registration and mode of taking the census, at the time they were made, may be applied with equal force to the plan adopted by this Government for enumerating the population. In some of the continental States, not only are the ages of the parties who marry noticed, and their relative number to those in single life given, but the mother is followed in her subsequent married life, and her age re-noted at every successive birth of a child, so that it is possible to ascertain the average number of children born to each marriage, and the age of the mother at the period of the births. The value of the information thus given is evident, and there is no reason why similar results may not be obtained in the United States.

The following tables exhibit the number at the several specified ages of each sex, who have been married in Massachusetts, for six years and eight months, beginning May 1st, 1844, and terminating January 1st, 1851:—

AGES OF MEN.	AGES OF WOMEN.																
	Under 20.	20 to 25.	25 to 30.	30 to 35.	35 to 40.	40 to 45.	45 to 50.	50 to 55.	55 to 60.	60 to 65.	65 to 70.	70 to 75.	75 to 80.	Over 80.	Unknown.	Totals.
Under 20,	476	183	22	1	..	..	..	..	..	..	..	..	..	..	6	688
20 to 25,	5664	8710	1159	112	19	3	..	..	..	..	..	..	..	..	79	15,746
25 to 30,	2080	6186	3131	397	71	13	3	..	2	..	..	..	..	..	67	11,950
30 to 35,	425	1637	1533	734	120	42	7	1	..	..	..	..	..	..	56	4555
35 to 40,	98	448	589	457	295	56	19	3	..	..	..	..	..	..	13	1978
40 to 45,	30	137	281	321	206	146	24	9	2	..	..	1	..	..	15	1172
45 to 50,	7	34	92	162	182	107	65	24	2	2	3	..	..	..	6	686
50 to 55,	1	17	40	64	103	104	74	39	10	2	..	1	..	..	5	460
55 to 60,	2	3	13	23	50	58	55	43	26	6	5	..	..	..	2	286
60 to 65,	..	3	2	14	19	44	51	50	24	16	1	..	..	..	5	229
65 to 70,	..	2	2	2	12	5	17	36	29	23	5	1	..	..	1	135
70 to 75,	..	..	..	1	4	10	4	9	6	15	4	3	..	1	..	57
75 to 80,	..	..	1	..	..	2	1	3	3	7	4	1	1	..	..	23
Over 80,	..	..	..	1	..	1	..	..	..	1	..	1	1	..	..	5
Unknown,	5	15	7	5	..	..	..	..	1	1	..	..	..	..	836	870
Totals,	8788	17,375	6872	2294	1081	591	320	217	105	73	22	8	2	1	1091	38,840

A similar table, including similar results, for Kentucky, for the years 1852 and 1853, are likewise subjoined:—

Ages of Men.	AGES OF WOMEN.														
	Whole No.	Under 20.	20 to 25.	25 to 30.	30 to 35.	35 to 40.	40 to 45.	45 to 50.	50 to 55.	55 to 60.	60 to 65.	65 to 70.	Over 70.	Unk'n.
Under 20	614	520	167	15	5	..	1	..	..	..	..	..	..	4
20 to 25,	4732	2577	1822	238	48	13	4	..	3	..	..	..	..	27
25 to 30,	2331	988	1024	251	46	10	1	1	..	..	..	..	..	10
30 to 35,	894	267	389	142	71	10	4	1	4	..	..	..	..	6
35 to 40,	672	83	186	105	49	33	8	4	..	..	..	..	..	4
40 to 45,	296	30	90	52	61	36	21	3	1	..	..	..	..	2
45 to 50,	200	8	46	39	33	39	17	5	9	2	..	..	..	2
50 to 55,	148	11	21	29	23	24	17	22	2	..	..	1	..	2
55 to 60,	77	2	7	10	7	16	10	15	3	5	..	..	..	1
60 to 65,	66	3	4	8	5	9	8	13	10	5	2	2	..	2
65 to 70,	35	..	3	1	2	5	7	7	6	1	1	2	..	1
Over 70,	29	..	3	1	2	2	6	4	1	4	5	5	..	..
Unknown	372	17	29	7	..	2	..	..	..	..	..	..	..	315
Total..	10,166	4397	3791	900	352	199	104	68	29	17	8	10	..	376

And also a table, based upon similar results in Belgium, for the year 1841:—

TOTAL MARRIAGES IN BELGIUM.

	Men.	Women.
Under 21,	774	2,831
21 to 25,	4,677	7,421
25 " 30,	10,067	9,082
30 " 35,	6,527	4,928
35 " 40,	3,636	2,791
40 " 45,	2,037	1,477
45 " 50,	934	753
50 " 55,	512	357
55 " 60,	310	126
60 " 65,	244	67
65 " 70,	112	28
70 " 75,	36	13
75 " 80,	8	. 2
80 and upwards,	2	—

29,876

The foregoing tables, showing the results of the marriages contracted in the States of Massachusetts and Kentucky, so far as the age of the parties is concerned, and adapted from the Belgium returns, exhibit in a concise and admirable manner, the age and condition of the persons who have contracted this relation. It is hardly possible to devise a tabulated form which shall express the facts so clearly and concisely as the one just given.

From the Massachusetts Returns it appears, that of the 38,840 females who formed marriage relations, 8,788 were under 20, 17,375 between 20 and 25, 6,872 between 25 and 30, 2,294 between 30 and 35, 1,081 between 35 and 40, and 2,437 above that age. Of the males, 688 were less than 20, 15,746 between 20 and 25, 11,950 between 25 and 30, and 10,456 above that age.

There are peculiarities which do not admit of tabulation, and yet are interesting. Dr. Curtis, in his remarks upon the marriages which took place in Massachusetts, mentions some of these :—

" Age presents also quite an interesting topic for consideration. During the twenty months we find marriages among persons of all ages between 13 and 91. The youngest individual married was a female of 13 years, several instances of which occurred. The youngest male was 16, who married a female of 19; the youngest couple was a male of 17 and a female of 14; a male of 20 and another of 25 married each a female of 13; a male of 19, one of 21, and another of 27, married each a female of 14; two males of 25 each, two of 28 each, one of 30, one of 35, and another of 47, married each a female of 15; and a bachelor of 50 married a girl of 19.

" Although the male was usually the eldest of the allied couple, yet many instances happened where the reverse obtained; thus we find a male under 20 married a female over 40; a bachelor of 24 married a widow of 42; a bachelor under 35 married a widow over 60; and another bachelor under 40 married a widow over 75. A female of 18 married the *second* time, and one of 59 married the *fifth* time. A male of 30 married the *third* time. One of 36 and another of 45 married the *fourth* time each. Among those at later ages in life we find a male of 81 married a female of 69; but the oldest couple married were Mr. Calvin Kilborn, of Princeton, and Mrs. Susan Saunders, at the respective and respectable ages of 91 and 70. He is a farmer in good health, of sprightly habits and good mental faculties, still remembering the scenes and " incidents of travel" which he experienced in 1777, when he went as a fifer at the Bennington Alarm. It seems worthy of notice that in this office, and almost side by side, are the official records of Mr. Kilborn's enlistment in Capt. John White's company which marched to Bennington in July, 1777, and also of his marriage in November, 1848, more than threescore and ten years having intervened between these interesting events. He has always been able to do the work on his farm to the present time, with but little assistance.

" The following statement will be found to possess interest by showing the number and proportion of marriages at the different ages of the sexes during the last five years and eight months, viz., since May 1, 1854, 7229 males and 7453 females, whose ages were not stated, have been omitted in the calculations :—

		Under 20	20 to 25	25 to 30	30 to 35	35 to 40	40 to 45	45 to 50	50 to 55	55 to 60	60 to 65	65 to 70	70 to 75	75 to 80	Over 80	Total
Whole No.	Males,	401	10,115	7941	2430	1203	748	486	322	218	172	95	67	29	5	24,232
	Females,	5871	11,313	3751	1329	723	450	260	174	99	47	38	14	4	1	24,078
Per Cent.	Males,	1.66	41.74	32.77	10.04	4.97	3.08	2.01	1.33	.90	.69	.39	.28	.12	.02	100.
	Females,	24.40	46.98	15.58	5.52	3.00	1.86	1.01	.72	.41	.19	.16	.06	.02		100.

" The above abstract indicates, so far as can be illustrated by an analysis of upwards of 24,000 marriages, the ages of parties to which were stated, that the probabilities of marriage under the age of 20 years are nearly fifteen times as great with females as they are with males, and that between the ages of 20 and 25 they are much nearer equal, though still somewhat in favor of the female; but after the age of 25, till death, the probabilities of marriage are about two to one in favor of the male.

"Again we perceive above, that of all females married, the chances that this interesting event will take place prior to the age of 20, are about as *one to four* of all the probabilities that they will ever marry; that is, when a female arrives at the age of 20 years and is unmarried, *one quarter* of the probabilities of her ever being married are gone. If she passes to the age of 25 unmarried, nearly *three quarters* of her probabilities are lost, and if she is unmarried at the age of 30, she has passed nearly *nine-tenths* of her chances of ever becoming a wife. The case is different with males, more than one-half of whose marriages occur subsequent to the age of 25. But the period of life between 20 and 25 appears the most probable of all the quinquennial periods of matrimonial alliances to both sexes."*

The returns from Kentucky show that of the 10,106 females who were married in 1852 and 1853, 4397 were under 20, and 3,791 between 20 and 25. From this it appears that of all the females whose marriages were returned, 43.24 per cent. were under the age of twenty, and 37.29 per cent. between the ages of twenty and twenty-five, or 80.53 per cent. under the age of twenty-five. In Massachusetts but 24.40 per cent. of the females were married under 20, and 46.98 per cent. between 20 and 25, or 71.38 per cent. under the age of twenty-five.

These tables indicate a very marked difference between the Northern and Southern portions of the Union, in regard to marriage, if Massachusetts

---

* 8th Massachusetts Registration Report, p. 99-100.

is to be considered a type of the former, and Kentucky of the latter, which must manifest itself in all the future movements of population, seriously affecting their births and deaths, and influencing in a very decided manner the relative probabilities of life among the natives of the one or the other sections of the United States.

A comparison, instituted by Mr. Shattuck, between persons contracting marriage in Massachusetts and Belgium, for the first time, from dates already given, shows the average age in the two places to be—

	Males.	Females.
Belgium,	29.47	27.43
Massachusetts,	25.84	22.69

The elements upon which this computation was made, are derived from the Massachusetts Returns for 1845, and those of Belgium for 1841.

A similar one, based upon the Kentucky returns, shows the average age at marriage to be—

Males.	Females.
23.98	21.03

These tables show that in Belgium more men and women marry between the ages of twenty-five and thirty, and in Massachusetts, between twenty and twenty-five, than at any other period of life. In Kentucky, more women marry below twenty, and more men between twenty and twenty-five, than at any other age. Massachusetts is thus made to occupy an intermediate position between Belgium on the one hand, and Kentucky upon the other. The average age at marriage is found steadily to decline, so as to present the remarkable difference of 5.49 years among the males, and 6.40 years among the females, between Belgium and Kentucky.

A natural deduction from these premises is, that as women marry earlier, the number of children will be greater, and the sum of those who attain to maturity less than in those countries whose marriages are contracted at a more mature period. How far this result may be modified by a lower latitude, and a consequent increase of temperature, the means are not at hand for determining.

The principle is well established in physiology, that the human body matures much sooner in warm countries than in cold, and that the female in the former reaches a physical development which enables her to assume the functions of a mother, at a much earlier age than in higher latitudes. In the tropical regions of Asia, for example, the female reaches a point of development at eight which in the more temperate latitudes of Europe and America is not attained until fourteen. A system of reasoning therefore, which would place the inhabitants of these extreme countries upon a parallel in this regard, would be fallacious, because as nature has in each surrounded the human species by a combination of circumstances, which are entirely different, the one from the other, so it has doubtless established a series of natural laws to govern and regulate the movements of the human race in each different latitude, or variety of climate under which they may be placed.

Were it not for this compensation man must necessarily have been restricted to one particular belt of the earth's surface, instead of covering it all with his footsteps, and claiming the whole for his dominion. A limit is thus defined to the animal and the vegetable kingdoms. The lion and the elephant are never found to inhabit the same latitude as the ox and the sheep, nor are the latter ever associated in companionship with the reindeer and the Polar bear. The banana and pine-apple never flourish in a temperate region, nor do the apple and peach survive transplanting to the frigid zone. In this extensive department of nature, a particular place is assigned to each distinct species of either kingdom, admirably adapted to the wants of its being, or the purposes it is intended to subserve.

Man alone is endowed with a capacity for universal migration. Possessing no natural covering of his own, he is enabled in each latitude to adapt to himself that which is best suited to the climate. In the frigid zone he invests himself with the skins of animals, covered with thick fur; in the temperate latitudes, he fabricates a clothing from the wool of the sheep; and under the influence of the intense heat of the tropics selects a light linen texture, or almost entirely dispenses with the use of external garments.

These analogies are introduced for the purpose of exhibiting the great variety of circumstances under which man may be placed, and to serve as a caution against too hasty a generalization. It is true that the limits of the United States do not embrace the extremes of climate and temperature to which allusion has been made; nor do the States of Massachusetts and Kentucky represent its extremes. It does, however, possess in this regard a range of latitude and variety of climate, not only more extensive than any other civilized country, but nearly equal to that of all the countries of Europe, whose governments possess a system of registration.

Moreover, as the changes of temperature are much greater in the United States than in those European countries, a knowledge of the movements of whose populations are revealed through their population returns, it follows that the changes of climate from warm to cold, and the reverse, are reached in traversing a less number of degrees of latitude in the United States than in Europe; and hence while Massachusetts has all the characteristics of a northern climate, without its greatest intensity, so Kentucky possesses, in a modified degree, the climatic influences of a Southern latitude.

It must also be borne in mind that the climate of Europe and the United States are so different as not to be represented by the same parallels of latitude, and it has hence been seen that notwithstanding their differences in this respect the South of France and Kentucky, as southern localities, and Sweden and Massachusetts as northern ones, bear a marked correspondence with each other.

If these observations have any force, they would lead to the belief that the striking differences which have thus far been seen to exist in the movements of the population of Massachusetts and Kentucky, are not accidental, but in accordance with the laws which regulate and control them respectively —that these laws have shades of variation as they are made to operate upon the inhabitants of various latitudes, and that similar results are not uniformly to be expected—that while nature has provided in the most wonderful manner for the maintenance of the species and the preservation of a just equilibrium among the sexes, it has adopted different formulas to accomplish this end for different circumstances.

This is abundantly manifest in the difference of the rates of mortality between town and country populations, and the manner in which after a high mortality nature repairs the loss by an acceleration of the functions of reproduction, so that the number lost by death is compensated for by the number of births. Now, if these differences are developed under different circumstances in the same locality, it is fair to infer that they are more likely to be developed in places whose latitude and climate have little or no correspondence with each other. Nothing short of an accurate and uniform system of registration applied to every part of the United States, and continued for a period sufficiently long to correct the errors which will unavoidably become associated with it can determine this question. In the meantime there is sufficient evidence to show that the laws which regulate the population of any given place in Europe, as Geneva, are not more admissible of general application in the United States, than they are in Europe, although a single place might doubtless be found where the identity of movement would be as exact as in those of the places already put in comparison with each other.

It is because these rules are not general in application, that whenever any considerable sum is at stake upon the expectation or value of life, observations are made from various points and comparisons instituted between them. Milne did not rest satisfied with the quiet little town of Carlisle, embosomed in the centre of rural life, in England, or the accurate observations of that excellent old gentleman who officiated as its medical man (Dr. Heysham), but extended his enquiries on the one side to Sweden, and on the other to the south of France, and after becoming enriched with the labors of Nicander and Wargentin, in Sweden, and Mourgue, Deparcieux, St. Cyran, and Duvillard, in France, and in his mathematical deductions by Euler, La Place and Halley, produced his valuable work on Annuities, which is chiefly important because its range of enquiry is general, and its deductions extensive.

The ratio of marriages to the population is found to vary in different places. The Massachusetts returns give an average of one marriage to every 102 inhabitants of the entire State. In Suffolk county, in which Boston is located, the number was one in 64; while in Worcester county the number was one in 104, and in Dukes county one in 151.

The registration report of Kentucky, in alluding to the number of marriages which took place in that State, says: "It appears that there were 7,430 marriages in the State during the year 1852, of which 5,105 are returned by the assessors, leaving 2,325 or 39 per cent. unaccounted for. We had, therefore, one marriage to every 102.92 white persons in the State. The proportion varied very much in different counties. In Harrison and Jefferson the proportion was one in 50.34, and 54.90 respectively; whilst in Simpson and Livingston, the proportion was one in 239 and 216 respectively."*

The clerks of the respective counties in the State of Kentucky, as of

---

* 1st Registration Report of Kentucky, p. 105.

many of the other States, issue a license authorizing the contemplated marriage to take place, which certificate is presented to the clergyman who performs the marriage ceremony. A record of the issue of the certificate is always made in the clerk's office, by which means it is possible to determine the number of marriages which have taken place. In this instance it appears to have furnished a check upon the records of the assessors, and shows that they failed to return 39 per cent. of the marriages which actually took place. The correction, it will be observed, is confined to the white population, and properly, because all the marriages noted were among this portion of the population; the laws of the State of Kentucky, and indeed of all slave States, not recognising any legal ceremony, nor requiring any registration or certificate, in marriages among the colored inhabitants. Similar omissions, as to numbers, appear to have been made in the succeeding year, so that it is probable that the number of marriages which actually took place among the white population of the State, in two years, was about 15,996, or one marriage to every 100 of the white population. In regard to those marriages actually reported, there appears to exist no reason to doubt the accuracy of the returns as to age, or at least that they form as near an approximation as can reasonably be expected.

As to the marriage returns embraced in the census for 1850, Mr. De Bow remarks: "The ratio of marriages is very nearly one person married to every two hundred persons, varying between the States from one to 316, as in Delaware, one to 150, as in New Mexico, as one in 192, as in Massachusetts, a sufficient proof of the incompleteness of the returns."* It was hardly to be expected that in this particular the census should afford perfectly reliable information, because the marshals whose duty it was to gather these statistics, entered upon their task, without previous guide or

---

* Compendium of U. S. Census, 1850, p. 104.

direction. The returns, as given below, although acknowledgedly incomplete, are introduced as the best standard of comparison with those gathered in the several States at hand.

States, &c.	Married.	States, &c.	Married.
Alabama,	3,940	New Hampshire,	2,613
Arkansas,	2,112	New Jersey,	3,719
California,	....	New York,	31,465
Columbia, District of	373	North Carolina,	5,275
Connecticut,	3,213	Ohio,	22,328
Delaware,	564	Pennsylvania,	19,858
Florida,	431	Rhode Island,	1,327
Georgia,	4,977	South Carolina,	2,005
Illinois,	9,183	Tennessee,	7,872
Indiana,	12,423	Texas,	2,232
Iowa,	1,824	Vermont,	2,653
Kentucky,	8,091	Virginia,	8,163
Louisiana,	2,890	Wisconsin,	3,015
Maine,	4,886	Territories { Minnesota,	39
Maryland,	3,703	New Mexico,	916
Massachusetts,	10,347	Oregon,	168
Michigan,	4,257	Utah,	404
Mississippi,	2,774		
Missouri,	6,989	Total,	197,029

Neither the marriage returns of Connecticut, which are included in the Registration returns, nor those of New Jersey, which are computed at 4,242, appear to be more reliable than those returned by the marshals, and included in the United States census, from which it will be seen by comparison they differ largely.

The returns of Massachusetts and Kentucky, as corrected, furnish tolerably correct information as to the relative proportion of marriages to their respective populations. It would be just to apply them to the whole Union, as fair representatives of distinct portions, which would give a ratio of one marriage to each 101 of the population. This proportion is much greater than among the populations of any of the European States, which have rendered returns, except Russia, to whose population in some respects that of the United States bears a strong affinity.

"Our returns (remarks the Rhode Island report) are inadequate to show what has been the real proportion of marriages to the population. But those who are acknowledged and recorded as having been made happy in this way, are, (if we take the population from the census of 1850,) in the last seven months of 1853, at the rate of one for every 91.99 in a year, and in 1854, one for every 70.46. From the whole population, however, we ought, perhaps, to subtract that of towns which made no returns of marriages, so as to base our calculation on the 'represented population.' Doing this, the ratio would be, for the last seven months of 1853, at the rate of one to 74.36 in a year, and for 1854, one person married in every 64.71. In the first report, it was one to 81.636. *

In England, there were living to each marriage, . . . 131 persons.
  Austria, " " " " "   . . . 124 "
  France, " " " " "   . . . 121 "
  Prussia, " " " " "   . . . 113 "
  Russia, " " " " "   . . . 90 "

---

* 2d Registration Report of Rhode Island, p. 23.

CHAPTER X.

MORTALITY.

The statistics of mortality are much more palpable in their immediate results, to those who do not directly concern themselves with the movements of population, than either those of births or marriages, and they have consequently not only attracted a larger share of public attention, but have likewise induced a larger amount of municipal and State legislation. There is scarcely to be found a populous town, in any country, marked by a high degree of civilization, which does not preserve a record more or less perfect of the deaths which take place among its inhabitants.

In most of the populous places in the United States, these mortuary registers cover a comparatively large number of years, and it is therefore no difficult task to ascertain the rate of mortality peculiar to each, and with some degree of precision the ages upon which this mortality falls. The outlets of human life, in the guise of various diseases, are likewise taken notice of, to a sufficient extent, to mark the influence of the locality, if any peculiarity exists, upon its inhabitants, and to determine the species of disease most fatal to its population.

In country districts, previous to the establishment of the system of registration, so far as it at present prevails, as a general rule, no mortuary records were kept, and there consequently existed no means of determining their mortality, or standard by which the relative value of life in town and country could be measured. The only information at present in existence concerning the number of deaths which take place in the rural districts of the United States, is to be found in the returns of the States which have adopted a system of registration, and the marshal's returns to the general government, included in the census for 1850.

As to the first of these means of determining the rate of mortality among the rural population of the United States, it is perhaps sufficient to say that in but seven out of the thirty-one States comprising the Union, is this system of registration in operation at all, and in some of those in which it does exist the returns are so imperfectly made as to deprive them of much of their value.

In regard to the enumeration, as made by the agents of the general government when taking the census of 1850, it is quite certain that it does not include all the deaths which occurred during the year prior to June 1st, 1850. This subject has already been alluded to, and some reasons have been given for fixing the number of omitted deaths at a certain increased ratio above those enumerated.

In addition to the bills of mortality kept by the various cities in the United States, and which furnish an excellent means of determining the error in the census returns, and of correcting it, the registration returns of at least two of the States supply valuable data, and constitute excellent standards of comparison. There is no more reason for refusing credence to the facts connected with the deaths reported by the takers of the census, so far as age, and name of disease are concerned, than there is to any other of the various departments of enquiry which came within their cognizance. In the collection of facts, as extensive as those of the enumeration of the population of a country embracing many millions of inhabitants scattered over a vast area, or of the various incidents connected with this population, whether pertaining to industrial statistics, or the increase of their numbers by birth, and their decrease by death, extreme accuracy is not to be expected. A certain margin is always left to that inseparable incident to all human affairs and all human reasoning—probability, which it is the province of mathematics to bridle and reduce to subjection.

Those fluctuations of population, which are affected by births and marriages, with much less reliable data than is furnished by the records of mortality within reach, have, it is thought, been determined with considerable precision, and there exists no reason why similar results may not be obtained so far as mortality is concerned.

The aggregate of all the deaths included in the mortality statistics of the census for 1850, distributed among the States in which they occurred, is given in the annexed statement:—

STATES.	Males.	Females.	Aggregate Deaths.	STATES.	Males.	Females.	Aggregate Deaths.
Alabama	4,812	4,279	9,910	Missouri	6,854	5,438	12,292
Arkansas	1,654	1,367	3,021	New Hampshire	2,038	2,193	4,231
California	794	111	905	New Jersey	2,513	2,952	6,465
Columbia, District of	427	419	846	New York	24,446	21,154	45,600
Connecticut	2,924	2,857	5,781	North Carolina	5,227	4,938	10,165
Delaware	644	565	1,209	Ohio	15,818	13,139	28,957
Florida	507	424	931	Pennsylvania	15,532	13,019	28,551
Georgia	5,176	4,749	9,925	Rhode Island	1,163	1,078	2,241
Illinois	6,336	5,293	11,759	South Carolina	4,207	3,839	8,047
Indiana	6,882	5,826	12,708	Tennessee	6,179	5,696	11,875
Iowa	1,140	904	2,044	Texas	1,641	1,368	3,057
Kentucky	7,983	7,050	15,033	Vermont	1,534	1,595	3,129
Louisiana	7,351	4,605	11,956	Virginia	9,735	9,324	19,059
Maine	3,882	3,752	7,584	Wisconsin	1,575	1,328	2,903
Maryland	5,127	4,494	9,621	Territories. Minnesota	19	10	29
Massachusetts	9,978	9,426	19,404	New Mexico	580	577	1,157
Michigan	2,423	2,092	4,515	Oregon	32	15	47
Mississippi	4,629	4,092	8,721	Utah	131	108	239

Of the 323,023 deaths included in the foregoing abstract, 172,878 were males, and 150,145 females. The difference between the male and female deaths being 22,733. The ratio per cent. of the male deaths to the males living being 1.46, and of the female deaths to the living females, 1.32:—

			To 100 deaths of both sexes.	
Whole No.	Males.	Females.	Males.	Females.
323,023	172,878	150,145	54.02	45.98

The proportion of deaths would be as 1,000 males to 919 females, or a difference of 81; which corresponds tolerably well with similar observations made in different countries,—the difference in some cases being somewhat over, and in others below, that observed in the United States.

This excess of male over female deaths is of almost universal occurrence. The returns of some of the States, however, show nearly an equal number of deaths for each sex, or, as in the case of New Hampshire and Vermont, a preponderance of female deaths over those of the male sex. In the former of these States the aggregate number of deaths was 4,231, of which 2,038 were males and 2,193 females, and in the latter 3,129, of which 1,534 were males and 1,595 females.

The returns of Massachusetts give an aggregate of 19,404 deaths, with a preponderance of male deaths. The registration report increases the number for 1849 to 20,423, of which 10,019 were males, 10,208 females, and 196 of unknown sex. The report, in commenting upon this peculiar fact, states: "We hear notice that a majority among the deaths are females. This is true in reference to the mortality of the whole State. In the country districts alone, however, the preponderance of female mortality is so much greater than it is in the whole State, that it casts the balance on the other side in the cities. If we knew the per cent which the number among the living of each sex bears to the other, in the cities and in the country, this might perhaps be accounted for in part, or in whole. It is to be presumed, that the female sex predominates in the State, and to a greater degree in the country than in the city. This is to be inferred from the fact, that although in 1849, among the births 52.06 per cent. were males, and 47.94 per cent. females, in the State, among the deaths under five years of age 53.82 per cent. were males, and 46.18 only were females; and that more males than females resort from the country to the city as residents, while the proportion of the sexes, between those who leave the State and those who enter it, is probably such as to produce no great effect in this particular."*

In the accompanying table the deaths which occurred under five years of age, and the aggregate for 1849, are so placed as to show the relative proportion of those who died under five years, and their sex, from which it would appear that although the whole number of deaths of all ages included a greater number of females than males, yet among those which took place in the first five years, the excess was among the males in the proportion, for the whole State, 53.82 per cent. to 46.18 of female deaths :—

Localities.	Births.				Deaths under Five Years.				Whole Number of Deaths.			
	Number.		Proportion.		Number.		Proportion.		Number.		Proportion.	
	M.	F.	M.	F.	M.	F.	M.	F.	M.	F.	M.	F.
State,	13,329	12,273	52.06	47.94	4169	3577	53.82	46.18	10,019	10,208	49.53	50.47
City,	5344	5106	51.14	48.86	2117	1875	53.03	46.97	4710	4617	50.50	49.50
Country,	7985	7167	52.70	47.30	2052	1702	54.66	45.34	5309	5591	48.70	51.30

"This abstract shows that the great excess of male mortality occurs in the earlier ages. Had we taken these who died under one year old, the excess would have been still greater. The disparity will be seen as follows:—

		State.		City.		Country.	
		Number.	Proportion.	Number.	Proportion.	Number.	Proportion.
Deaths under one year of age,	Male,	1994	66.13	996	55.14	998	57.16
	Females,	1558	43.87	810	44.86	748	42.84
Excess of Males,		436	12.26	186	10.28	250	14.32

* 8th Registration Report for Massachusetts, p. 109.

"The excess of males was, in every 10,000—

	Births.	Deaths under one year.	Deaths under five years.	Total of Deaths.
In the whole State,	412	1226	764	— 94*
In the Cities,	228	1028	606	100
In the Country,	540	1432	932	—260*

"There are various causes of death which press with unequal force upon the sexes. Those which seem to be the severest upon the *male*, are diseases of brain, except insanity; diseases of the lungs, except consumption; diseases of the heart, liver, most forms of fever, and the various causes of death, by violence. The mortuary tables of the last and former years also indicate quite clearly that those diseases which are more or less peculiar to the young, such as cholera infantum, croup, hydrocephalus or water on the brain, infantile diseases, and ulceration or canker, select a major part of their victims from among the male population. The majority of deaths from cholera were males, while those from dysentery and typhus were nearly equal as to sexes."†

The annexed table, which exhibits the relative proportion of the sexes at all ages for the year included in the estimate of deaths as given above, will enable a comparison to be instituted into the relative number of the living and the dead:—

Ages.	Females to 100 Males.	Ages.	Females to 100 Males.
Under 1,	....	50 to 60,	110.4
1 to 5,	98.2	60 to 70,	118.3
5 to 10,	99.1	70 to 80,	128.5
10 to 15,	97.7	80 to 90,	146.4
15 to 20,	114.6	90 to 100,	199.4
20 to 30,	106.4	100 and over,	225.0
30 to 40,	96.5	Unknown,	17.4
40 to 50,	99.8		

* Excess of Females.   † Ibid. p. 110.

Of all the 994,514 inhabitants of Massachusetts in 1850, 505,997 were females, and 488,517 males, being an excess of 17,480 females over males.

The population of the District of Columbia consists of 18,494 males, and 19,447 females, or an excess of 953 females. The deaths which occurred in 1849, as taken from the Census Returns, were 846, of which 427 were males, and 419 females.

For the purpose of enabling a more general comparison to be made, a table is presented containing a summary view of the progress of population in the Kingdom of Wurtemberg, which, like Massachusetts and the District of Columbia, contains a larger female than male population :—

WURTEMBERG.[*]

Year.	POPULATION.			DEATHS.	
	Males.	Females.	Total.	Males.	Females.
1833,	773,561	813,887	1,587,448	26,428	26,066
1834,	776,965	816,102	1,593,067	36,451	35,252
1835,	786,619	825,180	1,611,799	25,660	45,505
1836,	793,973	832,692	1,626,665	28,481	26,663
1837,	798,259	836,264	1,634,523	31,309	30,402
1838,	806,311	843,528	1,649,839	28,885	27,540
1839,	815,057	851,342	1,666,399	27,151	26,327
1840,	824,457	858,711	1,683,168	26,883	26,216
1841,	831,656	865,560	1,697,216	29,763	28,598
1842,	840,339	873,179	1,713,518	29,895	28,976

It will be seen, by an examination of these returns, that notwithstanding the fact that in Wurtemberg the female preponderates over the male sex, yet the largest number of deaths uniformly occur among the male portion of the population.

From these comparisons it would appear that in Massachusetts, and in all probability in the contiguous States, a different rate of mortality affecting the relative proportion of male and female deaths occurs, from that

---

[*] Count Beroldigen.

which is presented by the returns of the District of Columbia and the Kingdom of Wurtemberg, and which by comparison would probably be found more extensively to prevail.

If no further data were offered, than that of the record of the deaths for 1849, it might reasonably be inferred that the enumeration was erroneous and unworthy of credit; but the additional evidence furnished by the consecutive registration returns of twelve years, places this question beyond the possibility of a doubt. These returns invariably show that more female than male deaths occur in each successive year—thus of the 20,301 registered in 1853, 7,942 were males, 10,201 females, and 149 of unknown sex, being a preponderance of 268 female deaths. An abstract of the deaths of five years, including 1849, already alluded to, and 1853 just noticed, shows that of 92,174 deaths, the sexes of which were known, 45,855 were males, and 46,319 females.

Now, the uniformity of these results is too exact, and the period of time covered by the observations too extensive to admit of any doubt as to their correctness, and it remains to be seen upon what principle this apparent disparity can be reconciled. Mr. Shattuck has constructed a table for two years, which so admirably demonstrates this disparity, that it is inserted without comment:—

	To every 10,000 Males there were Females.		Showing a difference of
	Born.	Died.	
In 1844	9,508	11,241	1,733
1845	9,744	10,978	1,234

"It may be asked," he remarks, "what becomes of this difference? The answer is principally to be found in the greater number of males than females, which the State furnishes to people other parts of the Union, and to traverse the world. From the census of New York city, just published, it appears that 16,006 of its inhabitants were born in New England, and throughout all the Western States New England men are found. It would be an exceedingly interesting enquiry, how many emigrants have been furnished each year by Massachusetts. And if a good system of registration had been in operation, we should have been able to show how many have gone hence to spread the wholesome influence of the land of their birth in other States and other regions. If every 10,000 births furnish 1,250 emigrants, the 25,000 births which have been estimated to take place in the State annually would furnish over 3,000 to spend the remainder of their lives in other lands than that of their nativity."*

The census for 1850 gives the birth-place of each white inhabitant of the United States, so far as they could be ascertained; and that they have been arrived at with tolerable correctness is evidenced by the fact, that of 19,987,563 inhabitants, the places of birth of all except 39,146 are given.

Of these, the whole number of persons born in Massachusetts is,		894,818
Residing in "		695,236
" in other States,		199,582
Of which there are in Connecticut,	11,366	
" " " " Maine,	16,535	
" " " " New Hampshire,	18,495	
" " " " Rhode Island,	11,888	
" " " " Vermont,	15,059	
		73,343
In other States and Territories,		126,239

---

* Letter of Mr. Shuttuck to the Secretary of State of Massachusetts, p. 81.

From these statistics, as well as those already given, it is evident that the population of Massachusetts has been affected in the most serious manner by the extensive emigration and immigration to which it has been subjected. There is probably not to be found upon record an instance of a population in which these two causes have so effectually combined to change the population of an entire State as that of the one under consideration.

It is true, that in many of the States of the Union there exists a greater relative proportion of persons of foreign birth, than in that of Massachusetts, as in Wisconsin, where the number of these is 34.94 per cent., or in California, where it reaches 24.15, or in the older State of New York, where it amounts to 21.04 of the whole population, instead of 16.18 per cent., as in the case of Massachusetts. But notwithstanding the immense emigration from New York, which has gone to swell the populations of Ohio, Michigan, Wisconsin, Indiana, Illinois, and the other free States in the valley of the Mississippi, or that from Virginia and North Carolina which has gone to people the new slave States of the Union, and which in many instances exceeds in relative proportion that of the emigration from Massachusetts, yet in no one has the combined effect of the emigration and immigration produced such palpable results in this latter State.

How many natives of Massachusetts, in quest of a new home were males, and how many females, there is no means of determining. It is highly probable that many of those who changed their residence for that of neighboring States either went in families, or returned after a period to bring with them a partner who had engaged their affections before their migrations. Of these, the relative proportion of the sexes would doubtless be the same as was to be found in the State from which they emigrated. Among those who selected for themselves a residence in States more remote from that of their birth, the proportion of males was doubtless greater than that of females, because the occupations and habits of life of the former fit them for more extensive migration than the latter, who for the most part are found to change their abode under the auspices of their male relatives, either as parents or husbands.

Judging from the large number of marriages which occur among the residents of different States, as shown by the census returns for 1850, it is probable that comparatively few who were unmarried when they left home and made their residence in a remote State, ever returned to marry, and hence as the emigration from, is greater than the emigration to, most of the New England States, and doubtless embraces a larger proportion of males than females, the native female population must necessarily be in the ascendant.

Now, what effect these circumstances have upon the direct question at issue, the relative proportion of deaths among the two sexes, as made manifest by the returns of Massachusetts, is left for each to determine for himself. It may be proper to state, that although no entire registration district in England exhibits a larger proportion of female than male deaths, yet single counties, in rural districts, as Northamptonshire and Bedfordshire, among the South Midland Counties; Suffolk, among the Eastern; Wiltshire and Dorsetshire, among the Southwestern; and North Riding, in Yorkshire, are among those whose female deaths are more numerous than males. The Austrian Provinces of Illyria Corinthia, and Illyria Carniolia, as well as the Prussian Province of Westphalia, likewise show an excess of female deaths.

This excess of female mortality, wherever it exists, is exclusively confined to rural populations. The returns from all populous places, in the United States, show, that large towns are more inimical to male than female life, and that the proportion of deaths to the living of each sex among males is greater than among females. In this respect the New England States, where an excess of female mortality alone is found, do not form an exception to the general rule.

Another enquiry of equal importance with the one just discussed, is the relative proportion of mortality between the two sexes at different periods of life, for the purpose of elucidating which the following table is introduced, giving the number of males and females who died at each age throughout the United States, as returned by the census of 1850:

	Males.	Females.
Under 1,	29,569	24,696
1 and under 5,	36,349	32,364
5 " " 10,	11,549	10,172
10 " " 20,	13,760	14,485
20 " " 50,	48,773	41,734
50 " " 80,	26,511	20,840
80 " " 100,	5,152	5,020
100 and over,	173	190
Totals,	172,800	150,045

Although this table is freely admitted not to contain all the deaths which took place in the United States for one year, yet it is presumed to give a tolerably accurate account of those which come within the range of its observation. The omission is a general one, affecting some portions of the country more, and others less, as the marshals were more or less fortunate in procuring answers to their enquiries, or zealous in prosecuting them; but in no instance have the whole number of deaths which took place in an entire State been included in their reports. The relative division of deaths into male and female, and their distribution among the respective ages, with the exception, perhaps, of those which took place in the earlier years, correspond so well with the observations made by the registers of the States where notice is taken of the deaths which occur among the rural population and with those of other countries, as to lead to the belief, that they were returned, with tolerable accuracy, to the census bureau at Washington.

This table shows, in the aggregate, a preponderance of male over female deaths, in each period of life included, except that from ten to twenty years of age, in which the excess shifts to the female side of the table, to return again to the male side at the next period of life, which unfortunately embraces a stretch of thirty years, from twenty to fifty, in the early part of which, if a division had been made, it would have been seen that the female deaths were more numerous than the male.

Mr. Quetelet has given a table of the proportion of male and female deaths at different ages, for the town and country of Belgium, from which it appears that for every female death, there occurs the following proportions of male deaths, at the ages respectively named:—

Age.	City.	County.
1 to 2 years,	1.06	0.97
14 to 18 "	0.82	0.75
21 to 26 "	1.24	1.11
26 to 30 "	1.00	0.86
30 to 40 "	0.88	0.63
40 to 50 "	1.02	0.83
50 to 60 "	1.07	1.18
60 to 70 "	0.96	1.05
70 to 80 "	0.77	1.00
80 to 100,	0.68	0.92

From this it appears that at about two years the deaths in the two sexes are nearly equal; between the ages of 14 and 15, which is the period of puberty, the female deaths preponderate. Between those of 21 and 26 the male deaths are in the ascendant, from 30 to 40 the excess of mortality shifts again to the female side, and continues with them during the period of procreation.

---

* Quetelet, Sur L'Homme, vol. 1, p. 167.

L'influence des sexes est extrêmement prononcée dans tout ce qui concerne les décès ; déjà même elle se fait ressentir avant que l'enfant ait pu voir le jour. Pendant les quatre années de 1827 à 1830, on a compté dans Flandre occidentale 2597 morts-nés, dont 1517 de sexe masculin et 1080 du sexe féminin ; ce qui donne un rapport de 3 à 2 environ. Cette différence est considérable, et comme elle se reproduit dans les tableaux de chaque année, elle doit être attribuée à une cause spéciale.

Du reste, cette mortalité n'affecte pas seulement les enfants mâles avant leur naissance, mais encore à peu près pendant les dix ou douze premiers mois qui la suivent, c'est-à-dire à peu près pendant le temps de l'allaitement.*

During the decennial period from 1828 to 1837, the number of deaths in the Kingdom of Sardinia was 1,203,250

of which . . . 603,185 were males

and . . . 600,065 " females,

being in the neighborhood of 195 males to 194 females, or in the proportion of 100, 52 of the former to 100 of the latter.

" Il sesso maschile par dunque predominare nelle morti come nelle nascite, ma in ragion di gran lunga minore ; onde la popolazione maschile dello Stato viene crescendo con progressione piu rapida che la popolazione femminile ; avremo anzi opportunita di vedere in altro luogo che, mentre ne' primi anni del decennio che consideriamo la popolazione femminile eccedeva la popolazione maschile negli Stati di S. M., il contrario avviene dal 1832 a questa parte ; tuttavia si dee osservare, che le emigrazioni assai piu frequenti negli uomini che nelle donne, col diminuire il numero delle morti maschili avvenute in patria fan pur comparire minore del vero la ragione de' maschi a quella delle femmine nelle morti.

" Questo fatto del predominio delle morti maschili non é né eguale, né

---

* QUETELET, Sur L'Homme, vol. 1, p. 163.

costante in tutte le divisioni; esso ha luogo con diversa proporzione nelle quattro Divisioni che seguono, nelle quali si trovano:

Divisioni.	Mort. Maschi per 100 Femmine.
Torino,	101 12
Alessandria,	102 89
Aosta,	101 97
Nizza,	100 85

Nelle altre quattro divisioni succede il contrario, e si hanno:

Divisioni.	Morti. Maschi per 100 Femmine.
Savoja,	98 22
Cuneo,	99 95
Novara,	99 98
Genova,	99 95.

"Queste differenze cosi leggieri, ed ora in un senso, ora nell'altro, par che debbano attribuirsi a cagioni accidentali, anziché a niuna legge costante come quella che si osserva nelle nascite. Né si può dire che la mortalitá di ciascun sesso segua la ragione della rispettiva popolazione; poiché se cosi é infatti per le Divisioni di Savoja, Torino, Cuneo ed Alessandria, il contrario succede in quelle di Novara e di Genova, nelle quali muojono piú numerosamente, ed in quelle di Aosta e di Nizza, nelle quali muorono piú uomini, abbenché in esse il numero delle donne sia il maggiore. In generale la ragione de' due sessi nelle morti dipende dalla ragion loro nella popolazione, della legge di mortalitá per etá che a ciascuno compete, dal numero delle emigrazioni e delle immigrazioni, e dall'etá cui queste sogliono aver luogo.

"Havvi tra le cittá e le campagne una sensibile differenza nella ragion de' sessi nelle morti, essendo maggiore nelle prime la mortalitá degli uomini, nelle ultime la mortalitá delle donne. Fanno tuttavia eccezione le cittá di Torino e di Genova, nelle quali le morti femminili di gran lunga superano le maschili, tuttoché in entrambe queste cittá la popolazione maschile (comprendendo in essa la truppa di guarnigione, e per Genova la popolazione del porto) grandemente superi la popolazione femminile; infatti in Torino la prima sta alla seconda come 128 al 100. Ecco le tavole su cui le precedenti osservazioni sono fondate:

	Morti. Maschi per 100 Femmine.
Ne' Communi Rurali,	99 74
Nelle cittá in complesso,	104 87
A Torino,	94 13
A Genova,	95 66. *

It thus appears, from the observations deduced by M. Quetelet, from the eastern portion of Flanders, that during the four years intervening between 1827 and 1830, the number of male still-born, as well as those who died in early life, was largely in advance of the female mortality. The female mortality, indeed, does not, according to the facts deduced by this distinguished authority, begin to approach that of the male until the age of fourteen, and is not in the ascendant prior to the age of from twenty-six to thirty.

Although the observations made by the Royal Commission of Sardinia, just quoted, do not give the relative proportion of male and female deaths at particular ages, they yet furnish some valuable information in relation to the number of deaths in different places, from which it appears that while in some places, as in Turin and Alexandria, the female deaths were in the ascendant; in others, as Genoa, and Savoy, they predominated on the side of the males. The proportion of male and female deaths, in town and

---

* Inform. Statis. dalla R. Comm. Sup., Torino, 1843; Movito. della Pope., p. 664.

country, in Sardinia, appears to be particularly marked, being in the proportion of 99 males to 100 females, in rural districts, while it reaches 104 males to 100 females, in town. In this respect these observations correspond with those made in different parts of the United States, as well as the more northern countries of Europe.

The annexed table of deaths demonstrates that although the excess of mortality, in Massachusetts, is uniformly on the female side, yet during the early period of life, it is largely on that of the male:—

Years.	Sex.	Total.	Under 1.	Under 5.	20 to 30.	All others.
1852,	Males,	8,978	2,026	3,719	808	4,451
"	Females,	9,396	1,641	3,101	1,285	5,010
"	Unknown,	108	83	94	....	14
	Totals,	18,482	3,750	6,914	2,093	9,475
1853,	Males,	9,942	2,248	4,192	976	4,774
"	Females,	10,210	1,807	3,595	1,307	5,308
"	Unknown,	149	120	125	....	24
	Totals,	20,301	4,175	7,912	2,283	10,106
1854,	Males,	10,710	2,321	4,337	1,109	5,264
"	Females,	10,558	1,786	3,637	1,493	5,428
"	Unknown,	146	81	105	....	41
	Totals,	21,414	4,188	8,079	2,602	10,733
1855,	Males,	10,285	2,416	4,267	550	5,462
"	Females,	10,386	1,937	3,694	705	5,987
"	Unknown,	127	89	106	....	21
	Totals,	20,798	4,442	8,067	1,261	11,470
Aggregate,	Males,	39,915	9,011	16,515	3,443	19,951
"	Females,	40,550	7,171	14,027	4,790	21,733
"	Unknown,	530	373	430	....	100
	Totals,	80,995	16,555	31,072	8,233	41,78

The general experience of Life Assurance Companies, in Europe and in this country, is in exact correspondence with the results of the above table, and there seems to be no reason why the law of mortality in this regard should not correspond in the United States with that found to obtain in different European States. The experience of the Gotha Bank, in Germany, is pertinent to this subject :—

"Another feature which appears to characterise the class of persons who insure their lives, and results from Mr. Hopf's analysis of the Gotha statistics, is the much greater mortality of women at the earlier periods of life; in mixed populations, the reverse holds good. Thus, in the quinquennial periods, 26 to 30, 31 to 35, 36 to 40, the mortality of men is respectively 0.77, 0.88, and 0.98 per cent., while that of women at the same periods of life is 1.66, 1.79, 1.92. After 40, the difference ceases, and at the most advanced periods the females acquire an advantage over males. The Gotha Bank do not insure pregnant women, nor have they ever succeeded in determining a case of fraud on the part of a female; and yet, as the author observes, the numbers before us clearly prove that 'females understood better than males to gain advantage in the assurance.' The following is his explanation of the fact :—

'I think we must seek the principal cause of it in the circumstance that women, from the greater bashfulness peculiar to their sex, frequently do not communicate all their bodily infirmities and irregularities to their physicians, much less to others, and feel themselves much less under obligation to give notice to the assurance office of what they consider their own secret respecting the condition of their body.'

And again :—

'There is no doubt that a greater proportion of females who assure their lives at the younger years, die early. The deviation is too significant and too constant to be considered accidental. We are not able to explain it by any other supposition than by the circumstance that women feel internal hidden infirmities and defects in a higher degree than men, and have a presentiment of approaching danger in consequence of them, which impels them to assure their lives, or that they understand better and more skilfully than men to hide the true state of their health, and to deceive by it even their medical men.'

"It is, however, to be observed that the greater mortality of females below the age of forty does not apply in England, where the mortality of the two sexes is equal at that period of life. Our own experience would tend to show that this great mortality among females before the climacteric, in Germany, is due rather to the greater fatality in childbirth, than to the hidden defects adverted to. We throw this out merely as an impression obtained by inspecting numerous returns of foreign agencies, than as a fact, since nothing but the comparison of extended statistics can serve to determine such a question. We should have no difficulty in accounting for the circumstance, if proved to be based in truth, from the much more frequent employment of midwives during labor, in Germany, even among the higher classes, than among ourselves.

"We pointed out at the commencement of our remarks on the subject of life insurance, that insurers, as a class, present a much more favorable average duration of life than their uninsured compatriots. This, however, would not be the case, were it not for the surveillance exercised by the police of the insurance companies—their medical officers.

"Persons who feel the taint of any disease that may sap their vital power, are even more likely than others to insure their lives, in order to secure a provision for their wives and children. Were they admitted at the ordinary rates, the favorable averages spoken of as peculiar to the insured would soon be reduced below the average of the general population. It can only be by careful and conscientious appreciation of all the injurious influences to which mankind are subjected, and by a deliberate weighing of the circumstantial as well as the direct evidence bearing upon the health of an individual, that a medical examiner to an insurance company can completely fulfil the duties of his post. He has to guard against nervous anxiety in watching over the interests of his company, quite as much as against a laxity in examining the applicants for the benefits of the institution. The shock to a person in average health on being declined on the ground of some imaginary predisposition, and the injury inflicted upon him by thus refusing him the benefits of assurance, not easily obtained elsewhere when once refused, are matters for the serious consideration of the medical officer of an insurance company.*

The annexed table, prepared by Mr. Kennedy, late Superintendent of the Census Bureau, showing the per cent. of mortality in Massachusetts, Maryland, and England, among male and females, at each age, likewise illustrates this point :—Before introducing it, however, it may be proper to state, that as the officer upon whom the arrangement of the details of the census devolved, Mr. Kennedy bestowed much labor to perfect this new but important branch of statistical inquiry, and had the answers corresponded with the instructions in point of exactness, the information would have been everything that could be desired. Unfortunately, however, neither in the returns made by the marshals, nor in their collation afterwards, was the same care taken, as in the preparation of the forms adopted for their guidance. Nor is either he or Mr. De Bow to blame for the meagerness of the medical statistics which Congress felt so little interest in, as to order their publication after a tardy delay, on the sole condition of not exceeding 400 pages, instead of the elegant form originally contemplated by the officers in charge of the census office.

---

* British and Foreign Medico-Chirurgical Review, No. 35, p. 112.

ANNUAL DEATHS PER CENT—1850.

Ages.	Massachusetts.		Maryland.		England—1841.	
	Males.	Females.	Males.	Females.	Males.	Females.
0 to 5	7.105	6.052	5.466	4.875	6.838	5.860
5 to 10	1.168	0.983	1.041	0.855	0.955	0.922
10 to 15	0.452	0.573	0.477	0.606	0.509	0.542
15 to 20	0.572	0.831	0.605	0.757	0.718	0.801
20 to 30	0.998	1.170	0.896	0.938	0.949	0.942
30 to 40	1.253	1.346	0.991	1.146	1.080	1.121
40 to 50	1.513	1.325	1.884	1.249	1.410	1.308
50 to 60	2.067	1.654	2.433	1.712	2.230	1.938
60 to 70	3.482	2.960	3.405	3.285	4.232	3.761
70 to 80	6.767	5.762	8.977	7.221	9.150	8.378
80 to 90	15.000	13.470	15.157	12.280	19.850	18.850
90 to 100	35.240	27.540	31.132	23.430	37.390	34.570

The mortality returns of many of the States would appear to indicate that a difference exists between the northern and southern States, in regard to the relative mortality of the sexes in the middle period of life, from thirty to forty, and that the relative proportion of female deaths to those of males, was greater at this particular period in warm than in cold climates. The facts are not sufficiently numerous or well defined, to give anything beyond a mere shadow to this suggestion; but if, hereafter, under a more careful collection and analysis of facts it assumes a visible and substantial shape, it will furnish the starting point for many curious speculations which naturally suggest themselves to the mind upon its mere supposition.

Dr. Sutton, in order to exhibit the force of mortality upon the sexes, at different ages, formed a table, showing the number of persons of different sexes living in Kentucky, in each period of life, as designated by the census for 1850, together with the number of deaths, and the proportion of deaths to those of living at the periods given, as taken from the State Registration Returns for 1853.

Ages.	Number of Living.		Number of Deaths.		Deaths to Living 1 to	
	Males.	Females.	Males.	Females.	Males.	Females.
Under 1 year,	15,749	15,014	1,112	845	14.16	18.00
1 to 5,	71,938	65,981	974	867	73.85	76.10
5 to 10,	77,138	74,781	371	341	207.96	219.30
10 to 15,	77,713	65,196	224	236	346.93	275.88
15 to 20,	54,881	55,957	250	306	219.12	182.86
20 to 30,	89,336	82,782	507	620	176.20	133.52
30 to 40,	56,162	49,648	240	389	234.00	127.37
40 to 50,	35,567	33,011	224	263	159.22	125.52
50 to 60,	21,197	19,567	188	229	112.75	85.44
60 to 70,	11,058	11,173	189	164	58.56	68.13
70 to 80,	4,793	4,689	165	148	29.05	31.68
80 and over,	1,766	1,873	116	94	15.22	19.91

This table is best explained by the constructor of it, who remarks:—

"By examining this table closely, it will be observed that for the first six periods, the totals of deaths are greater than the sums of males and females. This is caused by there being one or more deaths at those ages in which the sex is not stated. In the census are a certain number of persons whose ages are unknown; and the same is true of the persons who have died; but no connection is presumed to exist between those thus returned in the census and in the assessor's book, for which reason they are both omitted in this table.

"This table shows an awful mortality during the first years of life—no less than one in 15.64 (or 6 per cent. of all children born,) dying within the first year. If we reflect, too, that, of necessity, there must have been many deaths which were not returned by the assessors; and again, that these infants were more likely to be forgotten than older persons, we shall be satisfied that this mortality, great as it appears, is yet far short of the truth. We must observe, too, that in every 100 dying during the first year, about 57 are males and 43 females. After the first year the 'value' or 'expectation' of life is much greater. Thus, more died during the first year than during the next four. Doubtless the chances increase as the time from birth increases; so that during the second period of four years, only one in 74.70 died; and the male excess is greatly reduced. During the third period, from 5 to 10, the chances of life have trebled from what they were during the second—the male excess rather increased. The fourth period, from 10 to 15, shows the greatest expectation of life—only one dying in 310. Here the chances of life have shifted, and the excess of mortality is among the females. From this time, the expectation of life gradually declines; until after the eightieth year, it is reduced to about what it was during the first year. The excess of mortality, too, continues with the females, until the tenth period, from 60 to 70, when it again returns to the males, and there continues to the end of the list.

" Since constructing the foregoing table, and writing the comments on it, I have examined carefully a similar table prepared by the Registrar-General of England, and find that his table corroborates surprisingly both the general correctness of my table, in early life, and the remark made as to the number of infants whose deaths have been omitted. From that table, it appears that instead of one child dying under one year in every 16 born, or 6 per cent. in England, 20.51 per cent. males, and 15.44 per cent. females die within the first year; thus demonstrating the enormous mortality of that period; and by legitimate inference, the great number of deaths among infants which are not returned in our report.

" In his table, as in mine, from births to the period " 10 to 15,' the excess of mortality remains with the males. In 10 to 15, and up to 30 to 40,' there is a very slight excess of male deaths; and through all succeeding periods, the excess remains with the males, and increases as age advances. Whether more extended observations will show an approximation of the proportion of ages and sexes to the English tables, we must leave for time to determine.

"I have looked into the relative mortality of the two races in early life, and find that of the 3,812 which are returned as having died under 5 years, 2,674 were whites, being one in 284 of the white population, and 1.138 were colored, being one for every 195 of the colored population."*

The remarks which preceded Dr. Sutton's table, relative to the mortality of the two sexes, at the middle period of life, is not only corroborated by it, but extended beyond to a point which it is thought will not be sustained by more general observations.

A comparison of the Swedish and Montpellier mortality tables will show that the difference in the relative mortality of the two sexes at this particular epoch of life, which has just been alluded to, as a possible characteristic feature of northern and southern mortality in the United States, also exists in the northern and southern counties of Europe, so far as these tables are an indication of the value of life among their respective populations.

The importance to be attached to these comparisons, between male and female life, cannot well be over-estimated, because it will be found that in proportion as the expectation of life increases in value, in like manner will the proportion of deaths between the sexes assimilate more closely to each other. Whatever cause tends to disturb these relations, as the hazards of early infancy, or the epidemics which prove fatal to later years, or the change of habit from a rural to city life, operates directly in abridging the span of human existence. A population whose aggregate age at death is large, is uniformly a population in which the relative number of deaths among each sex, in proportion to the living of that sex, does not differ materially; on the other hand, a population which presents a low aggregate age at death, is one which exhibits a great disparity in the deaths of the different sexes.

---

* 2d Kentucky Registration Report, p. 126-7.

CHAPTER XI.

LOCAL INFLUENCES.

The influence of locality in determining the rate of mortality, is made quite manifest by a comparison of the various registers kept in different places, and indeed is perceptible to most persons without this comparison. The various natural divisions of country into sea-shore and inland regions, extended plains and mountain elevations, fruitful valleys and rugged precipices, have each a very manifest influence over the health of those who inhabit them. Nor are those geological formations which divide the surface into alluvial and sandy regions, and scatter immediately beneath the soil which reposes upon them limestone, granite, sandstone, and other rocks, giving a whole belt of country to the one formation, and another belt to another, less potent in the development of the diseases peculiar to each, and which constitute the chief outlets of life.

But apart from these natural causes which are incident to each particular locality, and which spring from the surface of the earth, is that more potent one of climate, which often modifies those causes that give character to each especial district, and assigns to each latitude its particular type of disease.

Hence the inhabitants of so vast a country as that of the United States, which embraces almost every variety of natural division and geological formation, and, although possessed of a temperate climate, is yet subjected upon its southern and northern limits, in a modified degree, to the influences of a tropical and frigid one, are, as may well be supposed, subject to a great variety of influences, which operate in determining the rate of mortality, and fixing the relative value of life.

It is evident that these are not always the same, nor are they amenable to the same laws; and any standard of comparison which would assign a fixed rate of mortality to the whole United States must necessarily be defective and unreliable.

It might reasonably be expected that in each great division of country the period of life upon which death made its heaviest demand, after the passage of the infantile one, would be different; and indeed in infancy and the earliest years of childhood, the same result, in a more modified degree, might be expected. Among the diseases of maturer years, and especially those which fall with most intensity upon middle life, many are confined to certain well defined geographical limits, beyond which they rarely extend, so as to form a characteristic feature in the mortality of those localities placed beyond their confines.

Thus the intense autumnal fever, with its biliary complications and congestive type which prevails along the southern tier of States, and gradually loses its characteristics and intensity as it extends northward, is never seen in the New England States, or in those which skirt the Canadian border. Nor is the typhoid fever, which prevails in the northern States, especially in cool weather, a frequent visitor to the warm latitudes of Georgia and Alabama.

Both of these are so modified by a change of climate, as to develope themselves in an altered form, in the latitudes which intervene between these two extremes. Exposure to cold, which in a northern latitude would develope itself in inflammatory affections, intense in degree, but pure and simple in character, in a southern one, give rise to complications which seriously alter its character, and affect its mode of treatment and probable result. An inflammation of the lungs or their investure, which in a northern latitude would constitute a simple pneumonia or pleurisy, as far south as Virginia, would become complicated with an affection of liver, giving rise to bilious pneumonia or pleurisy, which is a much more serious disease, and requires a different mode of treatment.

These examples are sufficient to show the influence of climate and locality in the development of diseases, and in the modification of the same disease, and naturally lead to the expectation that as the causes which operate in each are not always the same, and the circumstances under which disease is manifested are diverse, so the results as developed in the demand upon life, would be different.

A striking evidence of the effect of locality and climate, in affecting the rate of mortality, is presented by the returns of the British army, whose duties, in guarding the immense possessions of that government, have made them the inhabitants of every variety of climate. The annexed table of the annual average mortality among the troops of this kingdom, is given upon the authority of Dr. Balfour, at the time Assistant-Surgeon to the Madras army :—

AVERAGE ANNUAL MORTALITY OF TROOPS AT DIFFERENT STATIONS, NATIVES OF BRITISH ISLANDS.

Station.	Authority.	Annual mortality per 1,000 troops.
New South Wales,	Marshall,	14.1
Cape of Good Hope,	Reports,	15.5
Nova Scotia,	"	18.0
Malta,	"	18.7
Canada,	"	20.0
Gibraltar,	"	22.1
Ionian Islands,	"	28.3

Station.	Authority.	Annual mortality per 1,000 troops.
Mauritius,	Reports,	30.5
Bermuda,	"	32.3
St. Helena,	"	35.0
Tenasserium Provinces,	"	50.0
Madras Presidency,	Quetelet,	52.0
Bombay,	"	55.0
Ceylon,	Reports,	57.2
Bengal,	Quetelet,	63.0
Windward and Leeward Command,	Reports,	85.0
Jamaica,	"	143.0
Bahmas,	"	200.0
Sierra Leone,	"	483.0*

It must be borne in mind that these troops were natives of the British islands, and consequently exhibited a much higher rate of mortality than the natives of the respective countries in which they were stationed; yet with this reservation, the table demonstrates most emphatically the effect of climate upon general mortality. The difference in the rate of mortality between native and foreign troops is shown by the annexed table, exhibiting the mortality of troops serving in their native countries. Thus among—

	Mortality per 1,000.
British regiments at home,	15.9
Maltese at Malta,	9.0
Hottentot corps in Africa,	12.5
Native Bengal army,	13.0
Native Madras army,	15.0
Native Ceylon army,	25.8
Annual average of native troops per 1,000,	15.2

---

* Journal London Statistical Society, vol. 8, p. 195.

The annexed extract from the statistical report of the sickness and mortality of the United States Army, is introduced to develope the same proposition :—

Regions.	Mean strength.	Number treated.	Deaths.	RATIO PER 1,000 OF MEAN STRENGTH.	
				Treated.	Died.
Coast of New England,	3,963	6,935	36	1,749	9.0
Harbor of New York,	9,387	31,397	183	3,345	19.5
West Point,	6,901	31,635	28	4,584	4.0
North Interior, East,	3,553	6,426	39	1,808	10.9
The Great Lakes,	10,346	22,784	140	2,202	13.5
North Interior, West,	7,230	16,707	77	2,310	10.6
Middle Atlantic,	6,299	14,262	117	2,264	18.5
Middle Interior, East,	2,456	6,373	36	2,594	14.6
Newport Barracks, Kentucky,	1,454	3,670	59	2,524	40.5
Jefferson Barracks and St. Louis Arsenal,	5,580	19,587	263	3,510	47.0
Middle Interior, West,	5,319	20,804	107	3.911	20.0
South Atlantic,	2,800	6,870	58	2,453	20.7
South Interior, East,	5,919	17,426	234	2,944	39.5
South Interior, West,	10,013	35,312	228	3,531	22.7
Atlantic Coast of Florida,	835	2,408	21	2 883	25.0
Gulf Coast of Florida,	2,299	10,262	70	4,463	30.4
Texas, Southern Frontier,	4,450	15,693	235	3,526	52.8
Texas, Western Frontier,	6,324	23,051	174	3,645	27.5
New Mexico,	5,873	11,738	139	1,999	23.6
California, Southern,	1,707	3,200	30	1,874	17.5
California, Northern,	1,599	5,420	70	3,389	43.7
Oregon and Washington,	1,831	4,253	29	2,322	15.8*

Neither of the results obtained by the returns given above, are to be taken as a standard by which to measure the relative value of life among the resident populations of the locality where the observations were made, because in addition to the circumstance that the life of a soldier is exposed to influences peculiar to itself, all of those noticed in the British army, and the portion of those in the United States who were stationed at southern posts, resided in climates to which they were strangers, and in which they were subject to influences not felt by the native residents.

It has been seen that the relative annual mortality of the different countries, which possess a record of the deaths that have taken place

---

* Mortality Statistics United States Army, p. 494.

among their respective populations, under the influence of the natural causes to which allusion has been made, and such artificial ones as they have chosen to surround themselves with, is quite different—the empire of Russia showing one death to each twenty-eight of its inhabitants, while in England the mortality declines to one in each forty-five. A subdivision of each country shows that mortality is greater in some rural districts than others, and in all presents a wide difference between town and rural life. Hence the law of mortality prevailing in Liverpool and the metropolis is not applicable to the rural districts either of the north or south midland counties, nor is that which defines the limits to human existence at each period of life, the same in France and Sweden.

In the United States, with the error of the census returns corrected, so as to give an annual mortality of one to each forty-eight of the inhabitants, a result is obtained which differs from each of the countries in Europe, inasmuch as it presents a lower standard of mortality. This standard of mortality, which after all is based somewhat upon speculation, is not by any means reliable, and it will consequently be necessary to arrive at the law which governs it by an examination of its individual details.

Parallelisms in different latitudes are not always to be expected; but, inasmuch as they have been found to exist between different parts of the United States and Europe, corresponding in geographical position, in other portions of this enquiry, it is anticipated they will be found in this; and although the results of the observations in no single country in Europe may be found to correspond with this, yet different parts of the entire continent may be selected, irrespective of the government under which they exist, which will assimilate to corresponding parts of the United States. The advantage of these comparisons has already become so manifest, that nothing further need be said in their behalf at the present time.

There is one circumstance connected with the climate of the United

States, which would lead to the belief that the correspondence between different localities in Europe and this country, apparently similarly situated, might not always be sustained, or lead to analogous results. This is the greater heat of the American summer.

The prevailing winds in Europe, as well as America, especially during the summer season, are from the west. In that portion of the United States embraced within the limits of the valley of the Mississippi, as well as in that stretched along the Atlantic sea coast, the effect of these winds, whose course is for an immense distance over dry land, with no intervention of sea, is largely to elevate the temperature. In Europe, the wind fresh from the Atlantic Ocean produces a directly contrary effect, and modifies rather than elevates the temperature. This effect is strikingly manifested upon vegetation. There is no part of the United States where the heat of summer is not sufficiently intense to ripen maize, and it consequently flourishes in the northern as well as the Southern States. In Europe, with the exception of the low latitudes, it is found impossible to bring this plant to maturity for the want of a summer heat sufficiently intense to ripen it. It is, therefore, reasonable to expect that in elevated latitudes, as well as in southern ones, the mortality, in July and August, when the period of intense heat culminates, will be proportionably greater than in countries similarly situated in other respects in Europe.

"The isothermal lines, first employed by Humboldt to measure the heat and cold of the earth, and to connect places having the same mean temperature, differ sensibly from the lines of latitude. We need not now enter into details how the earth's annual rotation and oblique motion, in relation to the sun, the centre of the system, fixes the tropical limits of the sun's apparent declination south and north of the equator, and produces alternate winter and summer on either side of the line, as it will be evident that the mean annual temperature obtained at different latitudes must decrease from the equator to the poles. Had the whole surface of the earth been uniform, presenting the like relations to radiant heat, unaffected by the unequal action of disturbing causes, the mean temperature of every point would have been in proportion to the radius of the parallel latitude. But the mean temperature of places, calculated according to Dr. Brewster's formula, from an equatorial mean of 81° 50′ Fahr., differs considerably from the mean obtained by observation. The mean temperature is usually higher at the same latitude in the Old World than in the New, and in north latitude than in south. Thus the isothermal line of 59° Fahr. traverses the latitude of 46° in Europe, but descends to latitude 36° in America. The general causes which disturb the symmetrical distribution of temperature, are the annual variations of the upper equatorial and lower polar currents of the atmosphere, the differences of its contained humidity, the unequal distribution of land and water in various countries, the peculiarity of the surface land, and its relative height above the level of the sea—all of which causes have more or less influence in determining the local temperature or climate of countries, and in fixing the isothermal lines that mark out the zones of disease."*

---

* British and Foreign Medico-Chirurgical Review, No. XXXVIII., p. 243.

CHAPTER XII.

NATURAL DIVISIONS OF THE UNITED STATES.

It has already been stated (page 18) that the territory of the United States is physically divided into three distinct sections, separated from each other by lofty ranges of mountains, and containing peculiarities rendering an examination of each a matter of the highest consideration. The first of these great divisions is occupied by the Atlantic plain and slope, which extends from the Atlantic to the crest of the Alleghany mountains, and is the oldest as well as the most populous section of the country. The second is embraced in the wide valley, bounded on the one side by the Alleghany, or Appalachain chain, and on the other by the Rocky Mountains, and is traversed by the Mississippi River and its tributaries. The third extends from the Rocky Mountains to the shores of the Pacific, and, with the exception of California, contains but a slender population, and is traversed by vast wastes of unexplored territory.

The Atlantic plain and slope, stretching from the river St. Croix upon the north, to the coral reefs of Florida upon the south, presents south of Cape Cod an unbroken front, upwards of one thousand miles in extent, to the waves of the Atlantic, unrelieved by any of those bold prominences which destroy the tameness of landscape. After passing Cape Cod, whose shores are low and sandy, northward, the highlands near the ocean, and the numerous harbors of Massachusetts, New Hampshire and Maine, open upon the sea in the midst of bold and picturesque hills, which contrast agreeably with the tame and monotonous scene of the more southerly coast.

Receding from the shore, this vast plain, at first level, becomes elevated into hills, which increase in boldness and diversity, until they finally rise into those lofty ranges of mountain peaks, which bound the Atlantic slope on its western side.

The breadth of this plain is not in all places the same. Beginning in New England by a narrow line, confined almost entirely to the sea-coast and the subjacent islands, it gradually expands as it proceeds southward, until in the Carolinas the mountains recede two hundred miles from the sea.

A well defined line of primary rocks, extending longitudinally through the whole length of this plain, from the New England States to North Carolina, marks the point of demarcation between the low and level plain skirting the sea shore, and the elevated land which finally loses itself in the lofty summits of the Alleghanies. This line of primary rock, which maintains an average elevation of great uniformity of between 200 and 300 feet above the sea, presents a visible barrier to the flow of the tide, and is marked in almost every stream that crosses it, on its way to the ocean, by a series of waterfalls or turbulent rapids.

The appearance of this chain of rocks clearly indicates that it once formed the shore of the ocean, and presented to the resistless beating of its waves, a long but not very elevated range of cliffs. The aspect of the plain, stretching towards the sea, is also strongly corroborative of this view. It is low, flat, sandy, and covered by an abundant series of alluvial deposits, and is furrowed out to the level of the tide in every part by a multitude of inlets which are not unfrequently associated with large patches of marsh, or salt-meadow land.

The upper part of the valley, divided by this line of rocks, is nearly of the same dimensions as that skirting upon the sea, and presents at the onset a range of gentle undulations which swell into bolder and bolder forms, until it sweeps over the blue ridge and rises into mountain peaks. It is principally composed of the older sedimentary and stratified primary rocks, and presents a fine hilly country, luxuriant in vegetation, rich in scenery, and possessed of a number of rivers, and a water-power of great value. Professor H. D. Rogers has called the alluvial range east of the line of primary rocks the Atlantic plain, and that west of it the Atlantic slope.

Most of the principal towns on the Atlantic are built along this line of demarcation, clearly showing the powerful influence exerted by geological phenomena upon the distribution of population. This line of primary rock may be traced from the city of New York, in the falls of the Passaic at Paterson, the Rariton at New Brunswick, the Delaware at Trenton, the Schuylkill at Philadelphia, the Patapsco near Baltimore, the Potomac at Georgetown, the Rappahannock near Fredericksburg, the James River at Richmond, the Brandywine near Wilmington, the Congree at Columbia, and the Savannah at Augusta.

The whole surface of the extensive territory limited by the Alleghany mountains, as well indeed as the greater part of the entire continent north of the Isthmus of Darein, is overlaid with a strata of earth and pebbles of evident diluvial origin, varying in thickness from ten to twenty feet, frequently leaving large surfaces of the rocky formation exposed, and as often burying them in an investure of thirty feet in depth.

West of this mountain chain, which not only presents a variety and beauty of landscape as grand and attractive as the loftiest peaks of the Alps or the Pyrennees, and is rich beyond calculation in its treasures of coal, iron ore, and other minerals, the interior valley of the Mississippi spreads by a wide and continuous sweep to the Rocky Mountains on the west.

These mountains, which are a continuation of the Andes of South America, and the Cordilleras of Mexico, obtain an elevation of fourteen thousand feet, rising into occasional peaks of upwards of sixteen thousand feet.

This valley is traversed from north to south upwards of three thousand miles by the Mississippi river. This parent stream receives the waters from numerous tributaries coursing through every portion of the valley, and forming highways upon which an immense commerce is carried. Cities of considerable size have arisen upon the banks of these rivers in various parts of the valley to accommodate the traffic, and the bottom lands in their vicinity have become covered by a comparatively dense rural population.

A very remarkable phenomena in the arrangement of this valley is the uniformity of its slopes. One of these reaches from the Alleghany Mountains to the Mississippi river, a second and larger extends from the Rocky Mountains to the same point, and a third gradually rises from the Gulf of Mexico to the head waters of the Mississippi, with so gradual an ascent as not to attain an elevation of more than 1,000 feet in the whole distance. The slope west of the Mississippi is regular, while that on the eastern side is occasionally broken into hills, and embraces the most fertile territory in the United States.

This immense valley contains vast spaces covered by marshes, and small lagoons, and others of equal extent, especially near the Rocky Mountains, whose sandy and arid soil affords but a stinted and scanty vegetation. Beneath this variety of surface reposes the formations of every geological era, from the alluvion of the Gulf of Mexico to the primitive rocks of the more northern section.

In all these varied formations the greatest order and simplicity are observed, and it is probably here, above all other sections of the globe, that the geologist can best read in its vast pages the history of the earth's geological formation. The primitive and metamorphic rocks, it is true, are seldom seen, and are only exposed by upheaval from their natural positions, but the lower silurian, the upper silurian, the Devonian and the carboniferous strata, present themselves in unvaried regularity over wide districts of country.

The extensive ranges of silurian rocks are, for the most part, composed of limestone, in every variety, from hard and dense, to soft and friable.

That these geological characteristics exercise a considerable influence over health, is well known. Their connexion is too immediate and self-evident to the medical man to require examination in detail. The prevailing type of disease is dependant as much, and perhaps more, on the predominant rock of the country, than upon any other cause. Climate, temperature, hygrometic condition of the atmosphere, and prevailing winds, may have much to do in influencing the general peculiarities of maladies in particular localities; but all these agents combined are incompetent to generate the cause which frequently dwells in the rocky formation. Where the substratum is composed of clay-slate the country is level, and the soil is in an especial degree retentive of moisture, and consequently ponds and marshes abound, and intermittent fever prevails. A limestone formation, especially of a friable species, is characterized by a luxuriant vegetation, a picturesque landscape, and a high grade of autumnal fever. In the region of sandstones the surface is hilly, and frequently mountainous, arid, and less productive, the streams are pure and rapid, and stagnant water is unknown. This is the region characterized above all others for eminent salubrity.

It will be seen that there is no section which does not possess local causes of salubrity and disease, entirely independent of the great geographical divisions into which the country, as a whole, naturally resolves itself. When a sufficiently minute series of statistics are obtained, the effect of these local causes will furnish the medical etiologist with interesting subjects of investigation. The Transactions of the American Medical Association contain some papers on local epidemics, which are valuable in this connection.

In forming an estimate of climate in temperate latitudes, such concomitant circumstances as proximity to the sea, or large inland bodies of water exposure to winds and elevation, must not be overlooked. Thus, in high latitudes, the sea-coast is always warmer than the interior in winter, and cooler in summer. The mountainous regions of New Hampshire and Vermont, although but a comparatively trifling distance from the coast, are so much colder during the winter season, that it is the constant practice of valetudinarians to leave those elevated situations during this inclement season to pass the winter in Boston, or other portions of the sea coast.

The following table, prepared under the direction of the Surgeon-General of the United States Army, is illustrative of this point:—

Places of Obsev'n.	Latitude.	Mean Annual Temperature.	Range of Thermometer.			Winter.			Spring.			Summer.			Autumn.		
						Dec.	Jan.	Feb.	March.	April.	May.	June.	July.	Aug.	Sept.	Oct.	Nov.
						34.95	23.31	31.87	40.58	54.66	61.94	69.27	72.98	75.57	65.48	54.45	37.90
						42.24	27.15	34.73	42.35	53.15	59.00	67.25	73.16	71.39	66.75	58.16	41.85
W. Pt.	41° 22'	51.56	101.	10	111	30.04			52.39			71.60			52.61		
Ft. T'll	41° 22'	53.10	88	0	88	34.71			51.50			70.60			55.59		

West Point, New York, is on the same parallel of latitude, and distant one and a half degree of longitude from Fort Trumbull (New London, Ct.) The former is inland, whilst the latter is upon the sea coast. Here, proximity to the sea, renders the winters 4.67° milder, and the summers 1° cooler, than at West Point.

This difference is still more manifest in that portion of the North American continent lying above the boundary of the United States. In Nova Scotia, which is nearly surrounded by water, the thermometer seldom indicates a temperature greater than 88° in summer, nor less than 8° below zero in winter; whilst in Canada, occupying the same parallels of latitude, the thermometer in summer rises as high as 97° and occasionally 100°, and the oppression is as great as in equatorial latitudes. In winter, a cold of 30° below zero, is frequent, and the thermometer indicates a range during this season of from 8° to 30° below zero.

The report of the Surgeon-General contains the results of a variety of observations made at different places for the purpose of marking the effect on temperature by proximity to, or distance from the sea, from which it would appear that the winters are 8.38° colder, and the summers 6.99° warmer, in the inland than on the sea coast.

It may be proper to remark that many of the inland military posts, are situated in the new country beyond the western border settlements, and are exposed to the bleak winds from the Rocky Mountains, which course without opposition across the open belts of prairie, forming so prominent a picture in this western landscape. Those who reside in these prairies believe, and perhaps justly, that the sun's rays obtain a greater intensity in their open and almost boundless fields, than where the scene is diversified by the green foliage and agreeable shelter of the thick forest. It is highly probable, therefore, that a comparison between localities less exposed, and in more cultivated regions, would not exhibit the same difference of temperature between the sea-coast and interior, as appears from the observations of the medical officers of the army.

The small numerous islands which dot the surface of the ocean on the shores of South Carolina and Florida, are famed for their salubrity and uniformity of temperature; while the interior in summer is parched beneath the intensity of a burning sun. The temperature here seldom attains a higher elevation than 80° or 83°, which, combined with the pleasant sea-breeze, almost continually playing over their surface, renders them delightful and healthy places of resort for the inhabitants of the main land.

The immense chain of inland lakes on the northern frontier, comprising a larger collection of fresh water than is to be found elsewhere on the surface of the globe, exercises, as may be supposed, a decided influence on the temperature of the country in juxta-position with them. It is estimated that these lakes contain 11,300 cubic miles of water, about half the quantity of fresh water on the globe, and reach for a distance of 1900 miles, covering over 94,000 square miles with water. Their depth is proportionably great—in some places, as in Lake Michigan, the sounding line having gone to the depth of 1800 feet without reaching bottom.

The effect on climate produced by proximity to ranges of mountains in the United States is very marked. The salubrity of those portions of Virginia, Maryland and Pennsylvania, lying at the foot of the Alleghanies, is doubtless in a great measure induced by the immediate presence of this extended chain of lofty mountains. The superior healthiness of this section of country is so famed, that large numbers of visitors from the lowlands and large cities, are in the yearly custom of resorting thither during the summer and autumn months, when the heat of town is most oppressive, and the malarial country most prolific of disease.

It not unfrequently happens, however, that the protection afforded by mountains against the strong winds, operates unfavorably on the maintenance of a wholesome atmosphere, and hence we often find, deep valleys in the midst of high and precipitous mountains without a proper outlet, oppressed by a degree of heat which is almost insupportabable. In those mountain gorges, on which the wind falls obliquely, and without sufficient force to sweep away the vapours arising from the surface, which constantly arise, laden with exhalations from the soil, an unwholesome moisture is ever present, the air stagnates and looses its vital properties; even the water is supposed to loose its healthy qualities, and the situation becomes in the highest degree prejudicial to health. Positions of this kind are seldom inhabited in the United States, owing to the extent of its territory, and the facility with which even the poorest persons can change their abode. In Switzerland and Scotland the melancholy effects of such a locality are rendered too visible in the miserable race of beings inhabiting them, who are the constant and incurable victims of scrofulous and rachitic affections, and who drag out a bare animal existence of mental imbecility and bodily suffering, oppressed by evils which they have neither the ability nor the inclination to cast off.

Elevation above the level of the sea exercises a decided influence over the climate of any particular latitude. The temperature of the atmosphere is found to decrease in successive and regular gradation as it leaves the earth's surface, so that in the ascent of the lofty mountains, within the tropics, the traveller experiences every change of weather, from the oppressive heat of the summer's sun on the plain below, to the piercing cold of eternal frost, on the lofty summit above. The variation of temperature has been found, with occasional variations, to equal one degree for every three hundred feet in temperate climates. This subsidence of temperature with elevation is doubtless dependent on the extreme rarity of the atmosphere at a distance from the earth, and the consequent facility with which it is permeated by heat, as well as the radiating powers possessed by the earth, which enables it to return the atmosphere a portion of the solar rays previously absorbed.

The atmosphere is condensed in proportion to the force by which it is compressed, and expands in exact ratio to the diminution of that force. It follows that the superincumbent strata of air, being compressed with greatest force in its most dependent part, and that dependent part being nearest the earth's surface, its density will there be greatest, and this density will diminish in exact proportion to the ascent of the column of air. Now, the air, when under a certain compression, has a certain capacity for latent heat, which is increased by a diminution of the compression, and diminished by its increase. If a column of air, at a certain distance from the earth, receive a certain number of sun's rays, and then be suddenly brought down to a position where it will occupy a denser medium, its particles being compressed, a portion of the latent heat becomes sensible, and is given off to surrounding bodies.

The following observations, made by Mr. Green, in an ærial voyage, exhibits this declension of temperature :—

"The thermometer at the earth's surface indicated a temperature of 74°

At an elevation of	2,952 feet, of	. . . . . .	72
" "	7,288 "	. . . . . .	70
" "	9,993 "	. . . . . .	69
" "	11,059 "	. . . . . .	45
" "	11,293 "	. . . . . .	38 "

making a difference of 36 degrees between the earth's surface and the highest elevation attained, or about one degree for every 311 feet of altitude. However, much more confidence is to be placed in the statements of Humboldt and Sir John Leslie, who believe the difference to be more marked nearer the surface of the earth.

The human body is supposed to be affected by the rarefaction of the air at great heights, as well as by a diminution of the temperature. On this point, however, there exists a diversity of opinion, some maintaining that all the unpleasant effects experienced in these ascents are to be attributed to the fatigue consequent on so difficult a journey; whilst others affirm that these effects are due alone to the character of the atmosphere. Under ordinary circumstances the equality of pressure from the air is so equally balanced without and within, that although a pressure is maintained equal to about 32,000 pounds, it is not felt. If any considerable portion of this pressure be removed, the bloodvessels, especially of the mucous surfaces, are more easily ruptured, and hence hemorrhages from the lungs and other parts of the body are more apt to occur. Strangers visiting Potosi, in South America, which is the most elevated town of any size in the world, being upwards of 13,000 feet above the level of the ocean, do not recover from the unpleasant effects produced by a rarefaction of the air at this height under a year, and pulmonary complaints are much more frequent among them than the inhabitants of the low country.

Taken as a whole, all the gentle slopes on this continent descend eastwardly towards the Atlantic, and the abrupt ones rise on its western aspect. In this respect a manifest difference is observed between this continent and Europe, which gradually declines westwardly towards the Atlantic.

This general configuration necessarily gives rise to a moister and more temperate climate in Europe than in America, in the same parallels of latitude. This effect would be much more obvious were it not for an admirable compensation made by the presence of the gulf stream and the trade wind that accompanies it. From this source, not only the Atlantic coast, but the Mississippi valley, which is exposed at its southern extremity to the Gulf of Mexico, derives a larger proportion of its moisture, and is equalized with that of Europe. The trade wind, fresh from the gulf stream, spreads itself along the whole Atlantic region and upon the slopes of the Alleghanies loaded with vapor obtained from the ocean, and not only supplies this part of the continent with a copious supply of water, but even distributes its favors, in a less degree however, to the Mississippi region, through its great inlet on the Gulf of Mexico. Were this great interior valley exposed to the southwest winds from the Pacific, instead of being shut out from them by the Rocky Mountains, its climate would doubtless be softer and more equable, and its influence over health and disease largely modified.

There is, perhaps, no concomitant of the atmosphere more immediately concerned in the maintenance of the functions of the body, more influential in the preservation of health, and more active in the production of disease, than moisture. Man constantly exists not only in an atmosphere of air, but likewise in one of aqueous vapor, which insinuates itself between the particles of common air, and pervades to a greater or less extent the entire etherial ocean, seriously modifying it, and influencing its action on the animate creation.

The human body is composed, in a great proportion, of fluid particles, which are incessantly in a state of motion—sometimes slow, and at other times rapid—that find a ready egress by means of the exhalent vessels, both from the external and internal open surfaces. In a dry state of the atmosphere, especially when combined with an elevated temperature, the exhalents are exceedingly active, and give off a greater amount of fluids than are required to be parted with for the due performance of the functions of the body. For this reason the desire for liquid aliment is manifestly increased in summer. Every one must have observed the difference in the amount of liquid taken in a dry or a damp day, at the same season of the year; indeed, this appetite, when not unnaturally created, and when the body is in a state of perfect health, is almost entirely dependent on the hyrometic condition of the atmosphere for the variation in its demands.

In Arabia and the interior of Africa, where the air contains comparatively little moisture, the inhabitants exhibit a dry and rigid muscular fibre, and possess an exceedingly small supply of fluids. In the British Islands, and the coast of New England, in our own country, where the quantity of moisture contained in the atmosphere is unusually great, the inhabitants exhibit a greater proportion of fluids in their organization than any other people on the surface of the globe. In Mexico, the table lands are celebrated for the dryness of their atmosphere. The rapacity with which it seizes on fluid particles is said to be so great, that the flesh of animals seldom becomes putrid, even during the heat of summer. The fluid portions combining with the atmosphere, the solid are preserved by means of this process of natural drying. The Indians upon the southwestern frontier resort to this method of securing their food by jerking the flesh of the buffalo.

The influence of moisture, as experienced by its presence or absence in winds, is very well known. Those winds which pass over a large extent of water are moist, light and warm, and exert a beneficial influence over the system, whilst those which find their way over a considerable tract of land are drier and heavier. In warm countries, the winds from land, freighted with the additional heat derived from the burning soil, and deprived of the greater proportion of their moisture, are dry, hot, suffocating, and are frequently productive of the most dreadful effects to those travellers, who, on the deserts of Africa, or the plains of India, are exposed to their action.

This aqueous vapor, so necessary for the due performance of the animal functions, has its force determined, and its quantity established in the atmosphere, by locality, temperature, pressure, and motion of the air. In its aerial form, vapor, like all the other constituents of the mixed atmosphere in which we live, is colorless and transparent; but in the act of condensing, it imparts to the atmosphere a certain degree of opacity, proportioned to the conglomeration of the watery particles. The *visible vapor*, arising from the condensation of the transparent portions of the watery atmosphere, becomes manifest to our senses, in the form of clouds, mist and fog; and when the collection is too large to be sustained by the buoyancy of the air, it descends upon the earth, in rain, hail, or snow.

The vapor in the atmosphere is derived from the evaporation of water at the earth's surface. This process takes place with greater rapidity at a high than at a low temperature, in a dry than in a moist atmosphere, in an agitated rather than in a quiet air, and hence a warm climate and dry winds are highly favorable to its production.

These general observations will enable the reader to understand why certain localities in the same latitude are different from others. With these characteristics of territory before him, he will readily comprehend why the same degree of latitude presents a great variety of forms of disease, some of which are referable to one condition of climate and others to another, and will be prepared to explain many apparently contradictory phenomena which present themselves in the investigation of the causes of mortality in so extensive and diversified a country as that embraced within the limits of the United States.

CHAPTER XIII.

INFLUENCE OF SEASONS.

The following table exhibits the number of deaths which occurred in each of the four seasons of the year, in each State of the Union:—

States.	Spring.	Summer.	Autumn.	Winter.
Alabama,	2,084	2,229	2,852	1,686
Arkansas,	756	718	933	548
California,	54	92	417	322
Columbia, District of,	236	253	189	146
Connecticut,	1,399	1,162	2,127	1,026
Delaware,	273	380	345	209
Florida,	226	252	247	174
Georgia,	2,559	2,535	2,692	2,051
Illinois,	2,492	3,333	3,649	1,742
Indiana,	2,765	3,540	4,160	2,039
Iowa,	523	526	605	356
Kentucky,	3,436	4,942	4,060	2,424
Louisiana,	2,784	3,505	3,053	2,514
Maine,	1,882	1,774	2,569	1,334
Maryland,	1,385	2,730	2,561	1,777
Massachusetts,	3,945	3,964	7,645	3,583
Michigan,	1,117	1,047	1,325	832
Mississippi,	2,089	2,371	2,645	1,460

States	Spring	Summer	Autumn	Winter
Missouri,	2,160	5,422	2,842	1,507
New Hampshire,	1,013	990	1,459	751
New Jersey,	1,463	1,750	2,175	1,037
New York,	10,101	12,444	14,843	7,602
North Carolina,	2,707	2,678	2,425	2,697
Ohio,	6,122	9,520	9,010	4,159
Pennsylvania,	7,649	7,517	8,129	4,042
Rhode Island,	473	520	817	520
South Carolina,	1,997	2,058	2,259	1,465
Tennessee,	2,924	3,818	3,039	2,244
Texas,	585	706	804	691
Vermont,	890	672	941	590
Virginia,	5,144	5,489	4,576	3,608
Wisconsin,	768	630	963	509
Minnesota,	6	10	7	..
New Mexico,	288	285	214	292
Oregon,	13	5	9	14
Utah,	56	97	30	52

From these returns it will be seen that the summer and autumn months proved more fatal than those of winter and spring. In most of the Northern States, as Maine, New Hampshire, Massachusetts, Connecticut and New York, the most fatal season was autumn; while in many of the Southern States, as Virginia, Kentucky, North Carolina and Louisiana, the period of greatest mortality was summer. This does not appear to be invariably the case, as in Alabama, Georgia, Mississippi and South Carolina, the number of deaths in summer and autumn nearly correspond, but slightly preponderate on the side of autumn.

The influence of Asiatic cholera, which prevailed as an epidemic during the summer of 1849, may have had some effect in changing the relation of the deaths to the four seasons in which they are classed, as it certainly had in the case of Missouri, where 5422 deaths are recorded in the summer quarter, and but 2842 in the autumn; but it is presumed generally to have had but slight effect, as the persons who were victims were usually of the humblest class in towns, and had but few friends to report their deaths to the authorities, by whom these returns were made; besides, the whole number of deaths reported as having died of cholera, in the United States, is 31,506, while it is known that 5,071 died from this disease, in the city of New York alone, and as many more in St. Louis. The great mortality which pervaded the whole valley of the Mississippi, from this disease, is, of course, not to be found in these returns.*

With scarcely an exception, the season of winter is to be found least prolific of disease. This diminished mortality does not appear to be confined to any particular section of country, but embraces with equal force the States located in the colder latitudes of the north, and the milder ones of the south, and contrasts in the most striking manner with the results of the registration returns of England.

From an examination of these, it will be seen that the heaviest demand upon life, in England, is in the winter season, when, according to the census returns, it is least severely taxed here, and that the periods of freest exemptions from disease there are those upon which it falls with greatest severity here. Now, while this table exhibits in the most positive manner the influence of the seasons upon disease, it at the same time shows clearly how very materially the law of mortality in England and the United States is at variance, and demonstrates the necessity of great caution in the use of the former when applied to an elucidation of the value of life in the United States.

This great winter mortality in England "exhibits," remarks the Re-

---

* Report on Asiatic Cholera in the United States, in 1849, by James Wynne, M. D. Appendix C to the Report of the General Board of Health, London.

gistrar-General, "in a striking light the fatal effects of cold." The degree of cold in the northern part of the United States is not only equal to that of England during the winter months, but far more intense, and if the mortality was due to cold alone, it should be far outstripped by that of this country, while in fact, with a lower depression of the thermometer than in England, this particular season is more healthy here than there. But the Registrar-General alludes to another cause which may operate with greater force in England than in this country, and certainly does so in the rural districts. This is "the crowding and privations to which a considerable part of the population is necessarily more exposed in cold than in warm weather."

A manifest difference in the habits of the inhabitants of the two countries is their relative division into town and country populations. Eight hundred and fifteen towns in Great Britain, in 1851, contained an aggregate population of 10,556,228 persons, nearly equal to one-half of the whole population, from which it would appear that the whole was nearly equally divided between those who resided in towns and those who dwelt in the country, giving a slight preponderance to the latter.

The aggregate town population of the United States in 1850, who dwelt in towns of not under 4,000 inhabitants, was about 3,000,000. Mr. De Bow estimates "that the village, town and city population includes about one-fourth of the whole," leaving as residents of rural districts three-fourths of the population, instead of one-half, as in England and Wales.

The statistics of neither country show any excessive crowding of the population into a small number of tenements, and will doubtless surprise those who have derived their information upon this point from a knowledge of some wretched and confined portion of a populous city in either country, where, notwithstanding the census returns, overcrowding does exist to a very alarming degree.

The number of dwellings in Great Britain and Ireland, according to the census of 1851, was 4,717,172. The number in the United States, in 1850, was 3,362,337.

The relative distribution of the population among those of the United States has been given in the census returns, from which it would appear that upon an average there was a house for every six persons, and ninety-three houses for each hundred families, which are thus distributed :—

Geographical Divisions.	Dwellings of white and free colored.	Families of white and free colored.	Ratio of families to 100 inhabitants.
New England,	448,789	518,532	19.01
Middle States,	1,046,131	1,175,612	18.01
Southern States,	423,681	426,691	17.88
Southwestern States,	359,511	366,802	17.65
Northwestern States,	1,041,332	1,066,777	17.54
California & Territories,	42,893	43,781	23.68
Total,	3,362,337	3,598,195	18.00

"Upon the average for the Union, there are 16.82 houses for every 100 white and free colored persons, or a little less than one house to every six persons, the ratio between the States varying from 15.17 dwellings to every 109 persons in Rhode Island to 25.6 in California. The proportion of families to dwellings in the Union is as 107.01 to 100. In Utah and Oregon there is one dwelling to every family; in Louisiana 100 to every 110; in Connecticut 100 to 114; in Massachusetts and Rhode Island 100 to 126, &c., &c."—*Compend. Census.*

In conjunction with this is placed a tabulated statement, embracing similar information concerning the several principal European States :—

Countries.	Number of Persons to each Dwelling.		Number of Persons to each Family.		Number of Families to each Dwelling.	
	1801.	1851.	1801.	1851.	1801.	1851.
Scotland, . . .	5.46	7.80	4.42	4.81	1.236	1.620
England & Wales,	5.64	5.47	4.69	4.83	1.204	1.132
Great Britain, . .	5.61	5.71	4.64	4.83	1.209	1.182
France, ...	....	4.85	....	3.97	....	1.222
Austria, ...	....	6.89	....	4.44	....	1.551
Prussia, ...	....	8.13	....	5.13	....	1.585

"The average number of persons to each dwelling in Ireland, in 1851, was 6.35; and in Belgium in 1846, 5.42.

The number of dwellings in Ireland in 1851 is stated at 1,047,735, making the total for the British empire, including the islands, 4,717,172. Adding the dwellings of the slave population, at least, on the average, as good as those of the operative classes of Europe, and estimating one dwelling for six slaves, the total dwellings in the United States will be 4,197,914. By comparison, one dwelling to every 5.82 persons in Great Britain, and one to every 5.52 persons in the United States."—*U. S. Census.*

It would seem from these statements, which must be considered as authentic, that ample provision has been made in each country included in these tables to provide a requisite supply of house room for its inhabitants; and it might reasonably be anticipated, that with a sufficient number of houses to accommodate six of the entire population in each, that excessive overcrowding could not take place.

The reports, however, of the English commission to enquire into the condition of large towns, as well as those of the Committee of the Legislature of New York, to enquire into the condition of tenant-houses in the city of New York, the Sanitary Committee of Massachusetts, and the report of the First Committee on Public Hygiene of the American Medical Association, show that the tendency of the poorer classes of the inhabitants of populous cities on both continents is to congregate in large numbers in the most confined and unhealthy portions of the places in which they reside.

The evidences are too manifest to admit of a denial of this fact, and it becomes a matter of importance therefore, in estimating the relative salubrity of a country, to ascertain what portion of this class of inhabitants are residents of town, and what portion reside in the country. The estimate of Mr. De Bow has assigned to three-fourths of the population of the United States a country residence. The justness of this estimate is confirmed by the statistics of the occupations of the free male inhabitants of this country over fifteen years of age, from which it would appear that of 5,371,876, whose occupations were defined, 2,400,583 were engaged in agricultural pursuits.

The registration returns of the respective States, although varying somewhat in detail, appear to corroborate the correctness of the census returns, in regard to the seasons upon which mortality makes the largest demands. Mr. Shattuck prepared a table showing the percentage of deaths in each of the four seasons which occurred in Massachusetts in the two years terminating with 1845, from which it would appear that the greatest mortality occurred in August and September, and the least in May and June:—

Months.	1844.	1845.
WINTER—January, February, March,	23.82	24.70
SPRING—April, May, June,	21.21	20.41
SUMMER—July, August, September,	28.80	29.86
AUTUMN—October, November, December,	26.17	25.03

In this table the winter has been made to terminate with the 31st of March, instead of the 1st of March, as it is presumed to have done, in the computation of deaths given in the census returns. The English report adopts the same arrangement of months, as that selected by Mr. Shattuck.

As a difference appears to exist as to the division of the seasons, it may be more satisfactory to define the months in which the mortality absolutely occurred, and with this view a table is presented, giving the number of deaths which occurred in the State of Massachusetts, during the three years terminating with January 1st, 1856, and the months in which they took place:—

Months.	Males.	Females.	Unknown.	Totals.
January,	2,296	2,344	10	4,650
February,	2,212	2,214	36	4,462
March,	2,555	2,621	43	5,219
April,	2,450	2,481	21	4,952
May,	2,227	2,239	38	4,504
June,	2,103	m 2,052	17	m 4,172
July,	2,780	2,679	32	5,491
August,	M 3,716	M 3,733	53	M 7,502
September,	3,548	3,524	59	7,131
October,	2,618	2,733	44	5,395
November,	m 2,092	2,116	24	4,232
December,	2,303	2,378	37	4,718
Not stated,	37	40	8	85
Aggregate,	30,937	31,154	422	62,513

A similar table is given for the State of Kentucky for the year 1853:—

Months.	Deaths.	Months.	Deaths.
January,	m 544	August,	M 1,053
February,	626	September,	906
March,	696	October,	802
April,	685	November,	631
May,	615	December,	723
June,	705	Unknown,	441
July,	984		

And likewise one tabulated in a somewhat different manner, but embracing the same information, for Rhode Island:—

	No.	Percentage.		No.	Percentage.
January,	328	6.83	August,	M717	14.93
February,	336	7.00	September,	542	11.28
March,	384	7.99	October,	403	8.39
April,	335	6.97	November,	327	6.81
May,	349	7.27	December,	314	6.54
June,	m 310	6.45	Unknown,	[6]	....
July,	458	9.54	Totals,	4809	100.00

"The mortality of Providence for fifteen years, as shown in Dr. Collins' tables, corresponded very closely with the above. The proportions of deaths in the several months were as follows:—

	Per cent.		Per cent.
January,	6.81	July,	9.55
February,	6.82	August,	M14.96
March,	7.67	September,	10.66
April,	6.76	October,	8.46
May,	6.99	November,	7.20
June,	m 6.45	December,	7.67

In connection with the mortality of the different seasons, as here presented, that which occurs upon the Pacific coast becomes important, as presenting a new arrangement of climactic influences, and a somewhat novel condition of society. The circumstances connected with the settlement of California are so peculiar as to render the facts derived from its vital statistics a matter of considerable interest, and it fortunately occurs that these facts, although embracing the results of but a single year, enables this comparison to be instituted.

The annexed table shows the monthly mortality of San Francisco from 1st June, 1855, to 1st June, 1856:—

	Males.	Females.	Still-born.	Totals.
June,	52	19	3	74
July,	82	32	7	121
August,	80	25	5	110
September,	84	29	5	118
October,	80	26	7	113
November,	75	36	5	116
December,	74	15	5	94
January,	82	24	9	115
February,	68	20	3	91
March,	63	15	10	88
April,	61	30	8	99
May,	60	20	7	87
Totals,	861	291	74	1,226

Dr. Sanger, from whose very excellent report to the Mutual Life Insurance Company, on the mortality of California, this table has been taken, adds:—"From this table, it will be observed that the greatest mortality occurs in autumn, and the least in the spring months—the former season having an excess of 73 deaths over the latter. The maximum of mortality is found in the month of July, when there were 121 deaths, and the minimum is 74 deaths in June. If we examine the table comparatively with reference to the causes of fatality for these two months, we shall find that the excess of deaths in July is partly due to accidental causes, and partly to an intensity of endemic, epidemic or malarious influences prevailing during this month.

"With respect to the seasons, Sacramento is similarly placed with San Francisco, in its mortality. We find, however, that the maximum of mortality took place in the month of November, when there were 30 deaths against the minimum of 15 deaths in February.

"From January to August, the mortality averages 17, and for the remaining five months over 25 monthly. From what has been stated, it is apparent that the greatest mortality, at Sacramento, occurs during the malarious season. This result is not surprising, because its location is such as to make it a favorite habitant for miasmatic disease. We regret that we have not before us the causes of the mortality for each month in the year, from an inspection of which we could arrive at more positive conclusions.

"There are important reasons why we should regard the exhibit of mortality in San Francisco as an excess, when compared in proportionate terms with the general fatality of the State. We shall have occasion to refer to the mortality of Sacramento, in confirmation of our opinion. Sacramento City is the principal resting-place on the great thoroughfare to the northern mines, and in reference to its position geographically, ought to afford just comparative views of the rate of mortality from malarious causes in this immense valley.

"In the first place, San Francisco is the gateway by which the large emigration constantly arriving here, as the commercial emporium of the Pacific, becomes gradually dispersed over the whole interior. The principal influx is from the Atlantic States, and of late years the routes *via* the Panama or Nicaragua Isthmus have been preferred to the more tedious journey across the plains. The almost malignant type of miasmatic fever, endemic, in the land crossings from ocean to ocean, is well known. To cut short premises, already familiar enough to the public, from the severity of past experience, we are having a population thrown upon us semi-monthly, to a greater or less extent, an invalid population, although with the improved facilities for transit not likely to suffer so much in the future.

"Then, again, we have had the usual history of scurvy and typhus attached to our emigrant ships in the long sea voyages around Cape Horn, from Australia, the Pacific Islands and the East Indies, under circumstances where a large number of human beings are crowded together in bulk, with limited accommodation for their wants, breathing a close and impure atmosphere, and provided, perhaps, with a scanty supply of nourishment, or one unsuited to the requirements of life at sea. The fatality from these causes has sometimes been frightful among the Chinese emigrants. For example, in the months of August and September, 1854, out of 4700 Chinese who arrived here, there was a mortality of 300 in port.

"In two of the vessels that arrived here during these months, there is a reported fatality of one out of five of the passengers during the voyage. From an inspection of the books of entry, at the Custom-House, there is reason to doubt whether the captains of ships have in all instances during this period made faithful returns of the extent of the mortality occurring on shipboard.

"Lastly, our city, in a sanitory sense, may be considered the hospital of the State. The invalid, from all portions of the interior, naturally enough finds his way to San Francisco, perhaps to seek a change in climate, or responsible medical advice, or to extend the facilities for successful treatment, and to secure for himself the full enjoyment of those comforts and personal attentions which his enfeebled condition demands, and which are most amply afforded in the metropolis of a new country.

"The mortality in our public institutions, the County Hospital and the U. S. Marine Hospital, illustrates the force of our observations. The former averages in the neighborhood of 170 patients constantly under treatment, the latter about 200, exclusively seamen. The combined mortality from these hospitals has been 16 per cent. of the entire mortality of the city. It should be remarked, that more than one-third of the patients received into the County Hospital are properly residents in other counties, who may come here voluntarily, or, as there is reason to believe, in many instances by the direct connivance of the local authorities to free themselves from the burden of their support.*

The registration returns of many of the States, among their other numerous defects, fail to indicate the months in which the deaths included in their reports took place. There is a sufficient uniformity among those which have not failed in this particular to show that the maximum of mortality in the United States is reached about the close of summer or the beginning of autumn, and its minimum about the termination of winter or beginning of spring.

This is precisely the reverse from what occurs in England and Sweden; the maximum in the latter country being attained in April, and the minimum in October, nor is the month upon which the maximum and minimum of mortality falls the same in every part of the United States. It has already been seen that a difference in this regard was indicated by the census returns; and were the registration reports of the various States sufficiently numerous, and accurate in detail, it would be possible to show an important difference in this respect between the great geographical divisions of the country.

As a general rule, however, the law of mortality which prevails in the United States is tolerably constant and uniform in attaining its highest altitude in that season of the year when summer merges into autumn, and when the heat is most intense. Nor does the law appear to be affected by a town or country residence, the prevalence or absence of an epidemic, ahealthy or unhealthy season, but pursues its course with great uniformity year after year, and invariably demands of this particular season the largest number of its victims.

---

* Report on the Mortality of California, by A. F. Sanger, M. D.

In order to illustrate the effect of locality upon the rate of mortality, the annexed table, showing the mortality of various cities in different parts of the United States, is introduced:—

					Per cent.
Boston,	39 years,	1811 to 1849,			2.45
Lowell,	13 "	1836 to 1848,			2.11
New York,	45 "	1805 to 1849,			2.96
Philadelphia,	34 "	1807 to 1840,			2.55
Baltimore,	14 "	1836 to 1849,			2.49
Charleston,	27 "	1822 to 1848,	Whites,		2.48
			Blacks,		2.64
			Both,		2.57
Savannah,	8 "	1840 to 1847,	Whites,		4.16
New Orleans,	4⅓ "	1846 to 1850,			8.10

This table, which was prepared with great care by Dr. Simonds, of New Orleans, exhibits the startling difference of 6 per cent. in the annual mortality between the healthiest and most unhealthy localities, and further shows that in each particular place a rate of mortality different from that of all the others prevails. Had the opportunity presented itself of ascertaining the difference between town and country in each of these localities, it would doubtless have exhibited a condition of things highly in favor of a country life.

But the most remarkable difference is, that which is exhibited between the cities of the north and south, as represented on the one side by New York and Philadelphia, and on the other by Savannah and New Orleans. In neither of these instances does there exist a means of comparing them with the rural population by which they are surrounded, other than such as is afforded by the census returns. Were there in existence State Registers, as accurate and carefully compiled as those of Massachusetts, by which this comparison could be made, they would doubtless furnish information, both curious and instructive.

Dr. Simonds, in his remarks on the high rate of mortality of New Orleans, says, that it has been in a great degree attributed to the recklessness of its floating population—to which opinion he is not disposed to assent.

"The only idea," he adds, "to be attached to the term floating population is that of persons who, though in the city, have not by length of residence acquired citizenship, or identified themselves with the city. This population must therefore consist of three classes—those who visit the city chiefly for pleasure and amusement; those who have visited us for the transaction of business, to dispose of their crops, purchase their supplies, &c., &c.; and those who have come here for the purpose of earning a livelihood, or of making a fortune, whose intention is to settle here and make it their place of residence, if they can do so consistently with their future welfare. The first two classes are here but for a few days, or at most a few weeks; they have left behind their ties of family or business that prevent a prolonged sojournment in the city; they are ready to flee at a moment's warning on an alarm of general sickness or a little personal indisposition; they reside at hotels and boarding-houses, in which, so far as my observation and inquiries go, there are but few deaths; and these classes, therefore, cannot contribute essentially to the mortality of the city.

"But is the floating population of New Orleans so much larger than that of other cities, as to account for a mortality double that of any other city? Has New Orleans a greater number of visitors in the pursuit either of pleasure or of business than New York? Certainly not. During a few months, say for half the year, New Orleans contains a large number of strangers, and also a large number of persons who claim citizenship and do business here, but who fly during the hot and sickly season to more congenial and salubrious climes. But New York is constantly thronged with visitors—its business season may be said to continue during the whole year—

and there is no season during which there is not collected together a large number of seekers after pleasure. Places of amusement, which are supported by strangers, are with us closed during a considerable portion of the year,—but not so in New York. Our hotels are deserted during the summer—theirs are always filled. But with us even a large portion of the private residences are closed for two, three, or four months of the year.

"The third class of the floating population consists chiefly of immigrants and adventurers, of perhaps but small or no means, who have cut off the ties that bound them elsewhere, and who, though but a short time resident here, are, to all intents and purposes, our own population. This class is enumerated in our census, pay taxes, contribute by their labor to the prosperity of the city, and will (if they escape the hand of death) become as truly citizens as seven-tenths of our present population, of whom indeed they constitute a large proportion. That this class contributes largely to swell our bills of mortality, is indisputable; but that the deaths from this class should be included in our calculations on the health of the city, is equally certain.

"If New Orleans really has proportionally a larger floating population than other cities, the reason is very obvious. Of the number attracted hither by the advantages of the city, a greater proportion die speedily, and consequently a smaller proportion live sufficiently long to become identified with the city. What length of time is requisite to change the character of those who come to reside in the city, from a floating to a permanent population? When this is settled, the record of deaths can be examined with reference to this question. Life Insurance offices recognise no fixed period of time, but require that the applicant shall have experienced the yellow fever, which on an average will be epidemic every three years. Our State laws require two years residence to entitle a citizen of other States to be considered a citizen of this State. The United States requires the foreign immigrant to have resided five years in the United States. The annual reports of the Charity Hospital have generally stated the period of residence as under or over three years. Let us say, then, that three years is a fair average to constitute the stranger a citizen in this respect. Of one hundred persons settling in New York in three years, nine will have died and ninety-one will become permanently resident; while of one hundred settling in New Orleans, twenty-four will have died in the three years, leaving but seventy-six permanent residents, the law of mortality of the general population being applied to the class of unacclimated. This statement is not strictly accurate—in fact, the difference would be very much greater, as those who maintain the position that our mortality is caused by foreigners, and that for natives and the acclimated our city is *very* healthy, must admit a much greater difference in the mortality of the newly arrived population. Again, suppose that on the 1st July, 1847, one thousand persons settled in each city, there would remain to be enumerated in the census on the 1st July, 1850, less than seven hundred and sixty persons in New Orleans, and more than nine hundred and ten persons in every other large city. Our neglect of sanitary measures, our indifference to the deaths of strangers, and our criminal disregard of the lives and welfare of those who settle among us, has done more to retard the advance of New Orleans than all the assertions of its salubrity can possibly remove.

" It may be said, however, that the floating population are foreign immigrants, who are merely passing through our city. Let us, then, examine the statistics of immigration, to see what light they throw upon this point. According to a statement published in connection with the reports of the New Orleans Charity Hospital, the total arrivals at New Orleans from foreign ports, coastwise, and by steamboats, during seven years, from 1842 to 1848, was 222,122—while the arrivals at New York from foreign ports alone during the same period, was 738,462. (Hunt's Magazine, XXI., 657.) But how do the arrivals at the two cities from foreign ports alone compare? During the year 1847 the total arrivals in the United States was 250,000, of whom 166,110 landed in New York—leaving but 90,000 for the rest of the United States. (Ibid.) Thus about two-thirds (66.44 per cent.) of all foreign immigrants landed in New York. Again, from 1845 to 1848 inclusive, four years, 104,293 persons arrived from foreign ports in New Orleans—number considerably less than the population of New Orleans and Lafayette by the late census—while 556,209 arrived in New York, being more than the population of that city at the last enumeration. The attempt to excuse the great mortality of New Orleans by referring it to the *vast* number of immigrants landed in our city, is not sustained by the facts."*

Are these ill-fated cities, in which mortality rages to such a fearful extent, dark spots in the midst of an otherwise sunny landscape, or do they bear in their high rate of mortality but a just comparison with the surrounding country? Dr. Barton, of New Orleans, whose exertions, in all matters pertaining to public health and philanthropic objects, have been unwearied, has prepared a series of tables, from the information furnished to him by the marshal, which divides the mortality of the State, as collected by the United States authorities among the respective districts in which it occurred, and gives for the State of Louisiana a detailed statement, which should have been extended to the whole Union :—

STATEMENT OF POPULATION AND DEATHS IN WESTERN LOUISIANA, 1850.

Inhabitants.			Deaths from Cholera.		Deaths per Cent.	
Free.	Slaves.	Total.	Free.	Slaves.	Without Cholera.	With Cholera.
90,312	121,158	211,470	103	561	5.09	5.22

EASTERN DISTRICT OF LOUISIANA, INCLUDING NEW ORLEANS.

Inhabitants.			Deaths from Cholera.		Deaths per Cent.	
Free.	Slaves.	Total.	Free.	Slaves.	Without Cholera.	With Cholera.
181,306	122,790	304,069	965	1040	3.23	4.34

* Simonds on the Sanitary Condition of New Orleans, p. 42.

These tables exhibit a mortality without a parallel in the United States, and show that there are causes in operation throughout the State tending to render it eminently unhealthy. Dr. Barton alleges that—

"The period adopted for taking the mortality of the State, with its census, has been an unfortunate one for Louisiana, for during the whole period embraced under the order to the marshals and their deputies for this enumeration, viz., the year ending in June, 1850, has been precisely one of those periodical cycles alluded to in the former part of this report as about the septem-decennial period for the return of epidemic cholera. Such has been the fact, and large mortality has resulted in the whole zymotic class (to which cholera belongs); for although I have been enabled to separate the cholera from the other mortality in most of the parishes, yet the mortality has been much larger in the congenerous diseases of this class, than usual; and many parishes of the western district of the State, where we know that the mortality is not in ordinary years more than one to one-and-a-half per cent., has been made, by this return, to show four, five, six, eight per cent., and upwards! This is to be deeply regretted, and the only remedy to be found is in the enactment of a registration law by the State Legislature, through which the actual sanitary condition can be made known annually." *

With the fact that the mortality of New Orleans has rarely fallen below four per cent., and has for the last four and a-half years averaged 8.10 per cent., according to Dr. Simonds' estimate, and according to Dr. Barton, for the entire period of its existence, 4.87 per cent., it cannot be considered otherwise than an extremely unhealthy city. Nor can a rural

---

* Barton's Vital Statistics of Louisiana, p. 21.

population, whose mortality reaches 5.22 per cent., as in the case of the western parishes of Louisiana, be called a healthy one. The remarkably low rate of mortality which was found to obtain in some of the eastern parishes of the State, and which appear more striking in contrast with the great mortality of the other portions of the State, would lead to the belief that an amelioration of its condition might be effected; but when, and in what mode, is left for those who are familiarized to each locality to determine.

To what extent the baneful influences which are seen to have foothold in Louisiana extend to the neighboring States, cannot, in the absence of more exact information, be accurately judged. It unfortunately happens, that in the contiguous State of Mississippi, which it is feared is more unhealthy than the returns have made it, the number of deaths were more carelessly noted than in any other State. That these influences do extend for some distance along the Gulf of Mexico, including the lowlands, which lie contiguous to its borders in the Texas, Mississippi, Alabama and Florida, and gradually lose themselves in the more elevated regions of these States, appears to be quite evident. It is quite certain that the section of country embraced within the limits just defined, is possessed of features peculiar to itself, and cannot be considered as a standard by which to characterize any other section.

Dr. Nott, of Mobile, in alluding to these characteristics says, that in the Southern States are high and healthy sand hills, placed in immediate contiguity with the rich alluvial lands of the rivers. The former are healthy, while on the low lands the most deadly malarial fevers prevail in summer and autumn. "Let us suppose," he remarks, "that a thousand inhabitants of Great Britain or Germany, should be landed at Mobile about the month of May, and one-third placed on the hills, one-third in town, and the remainder in the fenny lands around the latter. At the end of six months the result would be, that the first third would complain much of heat, would perspire enormously, become enervated, but no one would be seriously sick, and probably none would die from the effects of the climate. The second third, or those in the city, if it happened to be a year of epidemic yellow fever, would, to say the least, be decimated, or even one-half might die, while the resident *acclimated* population were enjoying perfect health. The remaining portion, or those in the fenny districts, would escape yellow fever, but most of them would be attacked with intermittent and remittent fevers, bowel affections, and all forms of malarial or marsh diseases, fewer would die, but a larger proportion would come out with broken constitutions.*"

Independent of the northern and southern climates, which have frequently been alluded to, and which find their types in Massachusetts and New York on the one side, and Kentucky and the Carolinas on the other, is this southwestern climate, stamped by characteristics bestowed upon it by its proximity to the Gulf of Mexico, and the peculiar character of the shore which borders it, and which are observed in their more complete development upon the borders of the Gulf, within the territory of Mexico.

It has been seen that each of these divisions possesses marked and characteristic features, distinguishing the one from the other, and rendering them amenable to different laws of mortality. The laws by which the two former are apparently regulated, correspond pretty nearly to those of similarly situated countries in Europe, but in no European country have features of mortality been discovered which would assimilate in character to the southwestern part of the United States.

---

* Nott and Gliddon's Indigenous Races, p. 364.

CHAPTER XIV.

DISEASES.

In forming an estimate of the comparative healthfulness of a county as a whole, or of individual portions of it isolated from the others, it is necessary to ascertain the chief diseases which furnish the outlets for human life, and their relative prevalence in the one or the other sections.

Without positive information concerning the ages at death, the information afforded by a simple record of the diseases which terminated life would be valueless, but with this information they become of the highest value; hence observations made in small places where the diseases can be accurately registered, are usually considered of more value in furnishing data for calculation, than in larger ones where the record is carelessly or inefficiently collated.

It has heretofore been found exceedingly difficult to arrange such a registration for diseases in large places where no possible information concerning them could be obtained, except such as the register afforded, as would clearly identify them, and admit of deductions being drawn from them; thus, Boston, New York, Charleston, Baltimore and New Orleans have each had their peculiar classification, frequently so diverse in arrangement as not to admit of comparison, without great caution.

This difficulty has been remedied within a few years by the very general adoption of Farr's classification of diseases, which all the States, and most of the cities, at present employ.

This classification divides diseases into two general classes of *zymotic and sporadic diseases*—the former term being used to designate epidemic, endemic and contagious diseases, and the latter those whose cause is found in the individual attacked by the disease. An example of a zymotic disease is given in Asiatic cholera, and of sporadic in dropsy. Zymotic diseases usually prevail in groups, attacking at the same time a large number of individuals, and are prevalent at one time, and absent at another. Sporadic diseases, on the contrary, occur singly and scattered, and under like circumstances are generally prevalent.

An additional division is made into twelve classes, which refer to the part of the body attacked by disease, one of these being placed under the head of zymotic, which is a class by itself, and eleven under the head of sporadic, thus:

CLASSES OF DISEASE.

1. Zymotic diseases.

SPORADIC DISEASES.

2. Of uncertain or general seat.
3. Of the nervous system.
4. Of the organs of respiration.
5. Of the organs of circulation.
6. Of the digestive organs.
7. Of the urinary organs.
8. Of the organs of generation.
9. Of the organs of locomotion.
10. Of the integumentary system.
11. Of old age.
12. Of external causes.

Since the adoption of this arrangement, which is very methodical, and at the same time quite simple, the returns of diseases have been much more reliable and easily classified. In collecting the number of deaths which took place in the United States, in the year 1849–50, this classification was given to the United States marshals and their assistants; and although they were not acquainted with the names of diseases and their mode of arrangement, yet, with the aid of this nomenclature, they were generally enabled to make a tolerably accurate return of the diseases returned or described to them.

This information has been collated, and classified in such a manner as to embrace within a few tables the names of the diseases, the season in which deaths took place, the age, sex, nativity, occupation and color of the deceased, from which it will be seen that the deaths from Zymotic diseases, were 131,813:—

Of which died of Cholera,				31,506
" " " Diarrhœa,				10,706
" " " Dysentery,				20,556
" " " Fever, general,				18,108
" " " Fever, scarlet,				9,584
" " " Fever, typhoid.				13,099

The deaths from Sporadic diseases and unknown, were,	192 210
Of which died of Dropsy,	11,217
" " " Cephalitis,	6,424
" " " Convulsions,	6,072
" " " Consumption,	33,516
" " " Pneumonia,	12,130

It will be seen by an examination of the chief causes of death, that a larger proportion of deaths are embraced in the slow and noiseless army of consumption, than in the more terrific and apparently fatal one of Asiatic cholera. It is quite certain, that the deaths from both of these diseases have been under-estimated, and probably in nearly a like proportion. The deaths from consumption, in Massachusetts, and the northern parts of Europe, usually exceed 2,000, out of every 10,000 deaths, and their relative proportion to the number of deaths in every country and under every variety of climate is very large. For the purpose of instituting a comparison between different parts of the Union, in order to ascertain the relative prevalence of this and other prominent diseases in each, the following table has been introduced, showing the number of deaths from the several causes named, which took place in each state named:—

	Ohio.		New York.		Maryland.	
	Deaths.	Per ct.	Deaths.	Per ct.	Deaths.	Per ct.
Apoplexy,	123	0.42	356	0.77	60	0.62
Cholera,	5,808	20.05	5,822	10.57	166	1.72
Consumption,	2,558	8.83	6,691	14.67	1,101	11.44
Dysentery,	2,563	8.83	3,691	8.11	607	6.30
Fever (general)	1,479	5.10	799	1.53	139	1.44
" Bilious,	201	0.68	330	0.72	264	2.74
" Congestive,	112	0.38	73	0.16	44	0.45
" Typhus,	750	2.59	1,037	2.27	360	3.74
" Scarlet,	1,301	4.49	1,028	2.26	561	5.83
" Yellow,	5	0.02	16	0.03	6	0.06
Disease of Heart,	137	0.47	545	1.19	129	1.34
Old Age,	506	1.74	1,393	3.05	278	2.88
Paralysis,	197	0.67	431	0.94	105	1.08
Pneumonia,	895	3.08	1,661	3.20	149	1.54
Scrofula,	101	0.34	177	0.38	35	0.36
Dropsy,	624	2.15	1,496	3.28	312	3.24

This statement would appear to indicate a greater prevalence of consumption and dysentery in northern, and of fevers and dropsical affections in southern latitudes. Were this bsolutely true, it is easy to see what important results would flow from an exact knowledge of the circumstances connected with the mortality of the different latitudes. The returns are not sufficiently accurate to warrant the assumption of such an important conclusion from them alone, but the fact that neighboring States in one latitude and contiguous States in another, should exhibit results which naturally lead to such an inference, is a sufficient reason for making a very careful examination of such facts as would sustain or overturn the conclusion.

The present mortuary returns of the general government and the States, do not supply sufficient numbers of these facts to warrant the establishment of a deduction from them. Did consumption prevail so much more extensively at the north than at the south, as these returns would appear to show, it might naturally be supposed that its cases would be increased, and their progress accelerated by the rigid season of winter, but an examination of the returns show that the effect of the seasons upon consumption is comparatively slight, and that if winter produces any effect at all, it is rather an ameliorating than an injurious one. The distribution of the deaths from consumption among the seasons, is as follows:—

Spring.	Summer.	Autumn.	Winter.
9679	8,742	7,982	6,800

Below will be found a table, embracing the deaths from consumption in Massachusetts for five years, terminating with 1855:—

Months.	Totals.	Percentage.	Months.	Totals.	Percentage.
January,	1,744	7.90	August,	1,884	8.53
February,	1,691	7.66	September,	1,947	8.81
March,	1,966	8.90	October,	1,850	8.38
April,	1,948	8.82	November,	1,739	7.87
May,	1,942	8.78	December,	1,869	8.46
June,	1,698	7.60	Unknown,	23	.10
July,	1,790	8.10	Totals,	22,091	100.00

The deaths in Kentucky from consumption, in 1852, were 956, or 9.20 per cent. of the deaths from all known causes. In 1853, the deaths from this disease were 846, or 11.45 per cent. of all the deaths. The months in which the deaths took place are as follows:—

Months.	Totals.	Months.	Totals.
January,	57	July,	75
February,	67	August,	69
March,	72	September,	67
April,	104	October,	62
May,	78	November,	62
June,	79	December,	64

From these various tables, it appears that the two maximum periods of death from consumption are in the spring and autumn, and the two minimum periods in winter and summer. In this respect the observations made in Kentucky corresponded very nearly with those made in Massachusetts. They likewise agree as to the age upon which consumption falls most heavily, which is between twenty and thirty years of age. One-fourth of all the deaths which occur from this disease are singled from those who are at this interesting period of life. The next most fatal period is that between thirty and forty, after which the proportion of deaths, as compared with other diseases, or with itself at these periods, rapidly declines.

The proportion of female to male deaths is greater than in most other diseases; in Massachusetts they bear the relation of 59.06 females to 40.80 males, and in Kentucky a proportion nearly corresponding to this.

But, although the characteristics of the disease are identical in both places, and exhibit a remarkable similarity in the season of the year, the period of life, and the sex upon which it falls, yet the relation which it bears to other diseases, as developed by these returns, is widely different, and appears to corroborate the census mortality returns.

Dr. Bowditch, of Boston, under the auspices of the Massachusetts Medical Society, is making a series of careful examinations throughout the State as to its origin and possible means of prevention, from which it is hoped many valuable facts may be derived, even should he fail to obtain any information by which its progress can be materially arrested. Were it possible to extend a series of similar observations, minute and accurate enough to determine its relative fatality to the number living or the aggregate dead over the whole Union, their importance would be greatly above the expenditure required for their prosecution, or the labor necessary for their accomplishment. The facts already elicited lead to the belief that results might be obtained, which would not only be gratifying but in the highest degree beneficial to humanity.

Next to consumption, dysentery is the most fatal disease of the northern States, and a very serious one at the south. Unlike consumption, its heaviest demand is made upon the earlier years of life—full one-half of all the deaths from this disease taking place in the first five years of existence. It also differs from consumption in the fact that it is amenable to the influence of the seasons. It prevails to the greatest extent in the months of August and September, and almost entirely ceases in the depth of winter and early spring.

In Kentucky, dysentery is so fatal a disease, that it is styled by the Registrar "the great scourge of the State." In 1852, there were 1,923 cases, which constituted 18.47 per cent. of the entire mortality of the State. During this year epidemic cholera prevailed to a considerable extent, and caused 722 deaths. In the following year, 1853, its intensity was considerably diminished; but it yet furnished a large item for the annual list of deaths—the number was 901. In some portions of the State it was particularly fatal; as an example, out of 113 deaths returned from Simpson county, 84 were ascribed to dysentery.

These two diseases select most of their victims from comparatively early life; and although no age is exempt from them, yet the period intervening between twenty and thirty years of age is that upon which the former falls most severely, and that from birth to five years, the one most susceptible to the latter. Nor are they confined exclusively or mostly to city life, but are found to prevail in the balmy atmosphere of rural districts, as well as the confined and vitiated air of town.

The returns of Kentucky, as made manifest in the registration reports just cited, and by the mortality tables of the census of 1850, exhibit a larger proportion of deaths from dysentery than the other States whose latitude is equally low. This corresponds very well with the prevalent opinion heretofore entertained by the medical men of Kentucky, unsustained by statistical evidence, and gleaned exclusively from observation.

How far the peculiar geological formation, upon which the soil of the greater part of the State reposes, which consists of a disentegrated grey and blue limestone, contributes to bestow this unfortunate precedence on Kentucky, or whether it in truth exists to the extent hitherto supposed or revealed by the returns of deaths, are questions that can only be solved by a more careful notation of the deaths occurring within the State, and the rendition of similar returns from other southern States.

Fever, in all its varieties, except scarlet fever, which is essentially a disease of childhood, and dropsy, fall with greatest intensity upon middle and advanced age. An examination of the census table, giving the ages at which death took place from particular diseases, as well as the returns made by the separate States, fully sustain this opinion, and at the same time show that a greater relative proportion of these diseases occur in southern than in northern climates.

The annexed statement shows the percentage of deaths which occurred in Massachusetts for a period of twelve years and in Kentucky for one year, from each of the causes above named :—

	Consumption.	Dysentery.	Fever.	Dropsy.
Massachusetts, . .	22.44	7.54	7.08	2.34
Kentucky, . . .	9.20	18.47	15.18	2.21

This statement covers a period sufficiently long, in the State of Massachusetts, to correct the errors of a single year, and without doubt gives a faithful representation of the average per cent. of mortality from each of the diseases included in the list. The period covered by Kentucky, however, is too short to be equally reliable; besides, in the year indicated, 1852, dysentery prevailed in an epidemic form throughout the State, and was unusually fatal. The comparison is the best at hand, and gives some conception of the relative prevalence of consumption, fever and dropsy, in each of the respective States.

The purpose, however, is not so much to show the relative prevalence of the one or the other disease, in these two States alone, as to indicate by their ratios of mortality, taken as types of a large extent of country, the particular classes of disease to which each are most exposed, and which prove the most destructive to human life.

It is to be regretted that no series of statistics of mortality, equally reliable with those of Massachusetts, are to be found in any southern State, with which a comparison might be made with more satisfactory results than the one just instituted. It is of the first importance to ascertain the relative prevalence of particular diseases in particular latitudes, because as each falls with greatest violence upon some particular period of life, it is possible to arrive at tolerably correct conclusions in regard to the most fatal age in different climates, by a knowledge of the diseases most common to them.

Thus it would be fair to infer, that if the diseases which have been mentioned as having most prevalence at the north or the south, as the case may be, really do prevail in either latitude to the extent which has been indicated, then the ratio of the population in either section, at particular ages, will indicate their presence or absence.

With the view to develope this proposition, a table giving the per cent. of the several ages of the white population of each of the States to the total population of these States, as deduced from the census of 1850, is introduced:—

STATES AND TERRITORIES.	Under 1.	1 to 5.	5 to 10.	10 to 15.	15 to 20.	20 to 30.	30 to 40.	40 to 50.	50 to 60.	60 to 70.	70 to 80.	80 to 90.	90 to 100.	100 & over.	Unknown.
Alabama	2.86	13.88	15.87	13.88	11.67	16.90	10.77	6.96	4.15	1.96	.80	.23	.04	.01	.02
Arkansas	3.37	15.03	16.27	14.25	11.13	17.53	10.77	6.51	3.22	1.36	.43	.09	.01	.01	.02
California	0.29	1.77	2.28	2.13	5.94	50.60	24.50	8.72	2.41	.50	.09	.03	.01		.73
Columbia, District of	2.63	10.66	12.96	11.57	10.67	19.70	13.91	8.65	5.41	2.64	.90	.28	.03		.04
Connecticut	2.07	8.84	10.56	10.44	10.47	19.36	13.59	9.94	6.96	4.51	2.33	.78	.08		.07
Delaware	2.74	11.68	13.94	12.54	10.92	17.83	12.77	8.51	4.94	2.65	1.14	.26	.03		.05
Florida	2.75	13.78	15.80	12.48	10.06	18.02	12.51	7.39	4.40	1.95	.66	.16	.03		.01
Georgia	2.91	14.10	16.06	13.95	11.24	16.95	10.28	6.93	4.03	2.25	.92	.30	.05	.01	.02
Illinois	3.14	13.57	15.35	13.34	10.96	17.74	12.11	7.34	4.00	1.70	.54	.11	.01		.09
Indiana	3.27	13.70	15.96	13.58	11.33	17.11	10.98	6.88	4.30	1.97	.69	.17	.03		.03
Iowa	3.18	14.67	16.13	13.19	10.47	16.86	12.54	7.17	3.72	1.51	.43	.09	.01		.03
Kentucky	3.10	13.47	15.36	13.27	11.15	17.62	11.03	7.09	4.22	2.30	1.00	.31	.05	.01	.02
Louisiana	2.70	11.86	12.97	10.94	9.05	21.65	16.64	8.36	3.64	1.46	.47	.11	.02	.01	.12
Maine	2.40	10.60	12.77	12.31	11.50	17.14	11.95	9.15	6.03	3.56	1.80	.59	.06		.14
Maryland	2.88	11.57	13.06	11.94	10.34	18.74	13.44	8.65	5.13	2.76	1.15	.30	.04		
Massachusetts	2.33	9.13	10.34	9.86	10.65	21.23	14.46	9.67	6.05	3.71	1.81	.58	.06		.12
Michigan	2.74	12.35	14.99	12.54	10.75	17.38	12.95	8.66	4.57	2.17	.71	.14	.02		.03
Mississippi	2.93	14.45	16.20	13.93	10.82	17.18	11.25	6.82	3.86	1.72	.62	.15	.02		.05
Missouri	3.31	13.61	15.37	13.39	10.90	18.28	12.12	7.05	3.73	1.59	.50	.12	.01		.02
New Hampshire	1.92	8.48	10.78	10.79	11.26	18.00	12.53	10.17	7.46	4.83	2.67	.96	.13		.02
New Jersey	2.76	11.20	13.04	11.84	10.76	18.33	12.68	8.71	5.55	3.21	1.41	.44	.04		.03
New York	2.47	10.58	12.21	11.07	10.78	20.25	13.58	8.96	5.39	2.95	1.29	.38	.04		.05
North Carolina	2.87	12.62	14.50	13.25	11.20	17.30	11.05	7.64	4.95	2.82	1.31	.40	.06	.01	.02
Ohio	2.87	12.80	14.72	12.88	11.16	17.76	11.64	7.69	4.55	2.59	1.02	.26	.03		.03
Pennsylvania	2.79	12.19	13.80	12.04	10.68	18.43	12.27	8.28	5.07	2.84	1.20	.33	.03		.05
Rhode Island	2.46	9.58	10.56	10.25	10.43	20.74	14.27	9.48	6.06	3.76	1.78	.56	.06		.01
South Carolina	2.35	12.77	14.78	13.46	11.02	17.23	11.22	7.71	4.98	2.72	1.23	.41	.08	.01	.03
Tennessee	3.03	13.69	15.71	15.04	11.75	17.00	10.21	6.79	4.12	2222	1.03	.32	.05	.01	.03
Texas	3.09	14.13	15.34	12.86	10.33	18.67	12.64	7.34	3.62	1.36	.39	.09	.01	.01	.12
Vermont	2.10	9.89	12.15	11.52	10.93	16.95	12.45	9.92	6.72	4.26	2.26	.76	.08		.01
Virginia	2.65	12.56	14.55	13.12	10.91	17.33	11.33	7.92	5.02	2.84	1.28	.39	.06	.01	.03
Wisconsin	3.41	13.42	13.85	11.14	9.43	19.13	14.67	8.13	4.33	1.82	.50	.10	.01		.06
Territories { Minnesota	2.78	12.44	12.78	11.91	9.29	7.55	28.44	16.08	7.00	3.01	1.03	.33	.08	.03	
Territories { New Mexico	2.00	12.30	14.18	11.42	11.41	20.47	11.77	7.13	4.67	2.76	.93	.52	.14	.07	.23
Territories { Oregon	2.37	13.27	14.07	10.77	9.18	24.28	14.43	6.55	3.26	1.13	.16	.02	.01		.50
Territories { Utah	3.81	15.30	12.04	12.07	11.70	19.02	12.00	8.09	3.75	1.71	.47	.04			
Total	2.75	12.06	13.83	12.28	10.89	18.55	12.36	8.13	4.90	2.67	1.15	.34	.04		.05

From this table it would appear that, as a general rule, the per cent. in the earlier years of life, to the whole population, is greater in the southern than in the northern States; that this difference disappears in middle life, from 20 to 50, when, unless affected by migration, the proportions become about the same in both latitudes, and that from this period the per cent. is steadily in favor of a northern climate until the last, when it returns again to the south. New Hampshire, which exhibits a smaller percentage of population in the earlier years, shows a largely increased one in the declining period of life.

This is, doubtless, in part due to the emigration which has for years been at work in draining the State of its more youthful population, while it has left a large proportion of the aged at home; but the universality of the law requires some more general and effective means than emigration to account for its action, and this is doubtless to be found in the relative prevalence in different latitudes or states of one or the other of the diseases through which the flood of humanity flows to its destined goal.

CHAPTER XV.

AGE AT DEATH.

One of the most valuable elements connected with mortality returns, is a correct enumeration of the ages at which death takes place, for, as it is possible by a knowledge of the diseases which usually prevail in a particular locality to determine with considerable certainty the ages upon which these diseases fall, so it is likewise possible, with the age at death, conjoined to those of the living, to estimate the comparative healthfulness of different places, and the probable diseases which prevail, and consequent value of human life within them.

It has already been seen, that the relative proportion of persons of a given age, to the whole population, differed very materially in different climates, and it has been inferred that the ages at death would correspondingly differ. This would probably be true if the population was stationary; but as it is affected by migration, the proportions cannot always be depended on, as many elements besides mortality conjoin to disturb these relations.

The first prominent feature that arrests the attention in an examination of this subject, is the great mortality that prevails among the young.

In all countries, and under all circumstances, in the same country, death makes its heaviest demand upon the infantile portion of the population; but although the demand is always greater upon this age than upon any other, yet surrounding circumstances have much to do in rendering it comparatively moderate or excessive.

Between the pure air of the country and the more confined atmosphere of town, or between the healthy portions of town, inhabited by the more opulent, and the confined and filthy courts in which the poor congregate, the differences are wide and startling.

In regard to this particular period of life, it must be admitted that the mortality returns of the census are not what they might be desired, and probably very largely fall short of the mortality. A reason for their want of accuracy in this report is easily found in the facility with which the deaths of young children escape recollection, while those among older persons are remembered. Hence, when a record of them is required, it might easily happen that those who were competent to furnish information were negligent without meaning to be so.

The larger part of the returns would seem to bear out the inference already drawn from the comparative rates of mortality among the young, manifested by the Massachusetts returns, and those of Charleston and New Orleans. From some, however, a different conclusion might be drawn; and as it has happened in more than one instance that the returns of two neighboring States, influenced apparently by the same causes, and subject to the same laws, yielded an entirely different result, it has been deemed most prudent to leave their guidance entirely, while investigating the facts connected with the mortality of infants, and the influence of locality upon it, and trust to those more scanty, but more reliable, records which the States in a few instances, and the populous cities in many, have placed within reach.

It is true, that these latter returns are confined exclusively to that phase of life which developes itself in aggregate numbers, and as the proportions between city and country mortality are quite at variance with each other, the same reasoning cannot be applied to both. The State returns are not numerous, and the mortuary records of the census in their application to infantile life are abandoned with greater regret, because they would, if reliable, have furnished most important data by which to elucidate the laws which regulate the infantile mortality of those rural districts in close proximity with the towns which have kept for a series of years bills of mortality.

In some portions of the country this infantile mortality is rather increasing than diminishing, and presents figures which are certainly large. Mr. Shattuck found that the infantile mortality of Massachusetts had increased in four years, from 1757 to 1762, or over 6 per cent., and that the deaths of children under one year, amounted to 17.62 per cent. of the whole.*

Dr. Curtis shows that 49.81 per cent. of all those who died in the cities of Massachusetts were under ten years while, in rural districts 41.11 per cent. of the deaths were under ten. "This," he properly remarks, "is a high rate to be sustained by persons who have not attained the termination of the tenth year of existence, and, so far as we have statistics, speaks more unfavorably for the cities than the rest of the State."†

In Charleston, the mortality under ten years, is 36.95 per cent., and in New Orleans it declines to 33.38 per cent. This would confirm the inference that a rigorous climate was unfavorable to the tender age of infancy and early youth, and that a warm one was that best suited to their condition. Dr. De Sassure and Dawson, however, in presenting a table of the

---

* Shattuck's Letter to Secretary of State of Massachusetts, p. 83.
† Eighth Registration Report, p. 116.

deaths which have occurred in Charleston, from 1822 to 1848, complain that the proportion of deaths under one year has increased from 15.59 to 17.32 per cent., or about the same as that of Boston. In the succeeding years, and especially the last few, the diminution, as compared with Massachusetts, was such as to render the whole mortality occurring, under ten years, 4.16 below that of the whole State of Massachusetts, and 12.86 per cent. below that of Boston.

From the Charleston mortality, which is inserted, it will be seen that the infantile mortality has been subject to great fluctuations, averaging from 1822 to 1836, 15.59 per cent., falling for the next period, from 1830 to 1840, to 13.09, and again not only rising to its former standard, but surpassing it, and assuming an attitude of 17.32 per cent.

The proportion of this mortality, between the races, is as follows:

	First Period.	Second Period.	Third Period.
White,	9.11	7.70	10.82
Black,	21.07	17.24	21.64

The average age at death has been considered so good a test for the comparative healthfulness of a country, that the States of Massachusetts, Kentucky and Rhode Island have taken good care, in tabulating the returns made under their respective registration acts, to ascertain and record the average age at death with considerable precision. The process of ascertaining the average age at death is simple, and consists in adding up the sum of the ages of those who die, and dividing the aggregate among the number of deaths.

This means of determining the relative health of a given population has been in use for a long period, and was in fact employed before any enumerations were made of the living. It is liable to very material errors, when applied to a population as fluctuating as that of the United States, which have been ably pointed out by Mr. Farr:—

"Take a street (C) in a town where, from the erection of new factories, or from any new field of labor being thrown open, a considerable number of young men and women have been attracted within the last 10 or 15 years; there is a demand for the labor of children; marriages take place; nearly all the young couples have children, two, three, or four in a family. Take another street (D), inhabited by artisans, whose business and numbers have remained nearly stationary, and tradespeople who have succeeded to old shops established by their fathers;—suppose the salubrity of the two streets, and the rate of mortality at the corresponding ages, the same,—it is evident that as the street C contains no old people, and the mortality in the first two or three years is always relatively high, the deaths registered will be at early ages—the mean age at death low; while in the street D, the deaths will many of them be at old ages, and the mean age at death relatively high. If all the inhabitants of the two streets died in one year, the mortality would be the same. Yet the mean age at death would differ in the same ratio as the mean age of the living. The same results would be produced by the death of *one*-thirtieth of the inhabitants in each street. The cases which have been put will enable us to understand such a case as is said to have occurred in Leicester, where the mean age at death was $13\frac{1}{2}$ years in the undrained streets, and $23\frac{1}{2}$ in the drained streets. That the real mortality was higher in the one class of streets than in the other, is probable; but this is not proved by the method, for the *undrained streets* may be new streets, inhabited by young people—a part of the 8,600 in 46,000 not born in Leicestershire; while the drained streets may be old streets inhabited by the old inhabitants of the towns.* On account of the system of compensation which it involves, the method of comparing the total deaths to the population of the streets gives results nearer the truth;

---

* I find, upon turning to the Census Returns, that the population of some of the new and old streets in Leicester differ in the manner described.

but no one acquainted with inquiries of the kind would place much confidence in any other method, as applied to *particular streets* or *small districts*, than that upon which the Life Table is founded—the comparison of the numbers living with the numbers born and dying at the several periods of life. In the Registrar-General's Report, the mortality is only given for statistical districts of an average population of 50,000.

"The mean age at death in the districts of the metropolis furnishes a series of very striking illustrations of the errors of the method: according to which *Greenwich* is the healthiest district in the metropolis; and would be placed first in a table of salubrity, as the mean age at death is 36 years in Greenwich, and only 31 in Hackney, 31 in St. George, Hanover-square. This result is produced by the accumulation of old men in Greenwich Hospital,* who, of course, die at advanced ages, and make the mean age at death high. Supposing the mortality among the old veterans to be the same as the mortality of the general population, it is evident that the living at 60–70–80, &c., would be increased as much as the dying, and that the method of comparing the deaths with the living would give true results. Rotherhithe, according to the same method, is healthier than Islington, Marylebone, and Pancras: in Whitechapel the mean age at death is 26 years; it is placed therefore higher than St. James's district, comprising the lower end of Regent-street, and higher than the wealthy City of London, in in which the mean age at death is only 25 years; an effect to be ascribed partly to the City of London workhouse for old people at Peckham, which is also one of the causes why the mean age at death is 25 years in the city, and 34 years in Camberwell. The 'mean age at death' is 21 years in St. Saviour, and 30 in St. Olave. That these results are absurd must be evident to all who are acquainted with the subject." †

---

* The deaths of 291 pensioners were registered in 1841; the total deaths in the Greenwich District were 2198.

† 6th Registrar-General's Report, p. 575.

There is probably no country to which these remarks are more applicable than to the United States. It is asserted by Mr. Farr that the population in England is so much affected by migration as seriously to interfere with the results of the average age at death, or the mean age at death, which is but another form for expressing the same idea. But the fluctuations of population in England are trivial, when compared to those that take place in the United States. Not only is the amount of immigration largely in advance of that of any other country, whose statistics of population are known, but the changes of the native inhabitants from place to place are much greater than those of any other people.

The restless and indomitable spirit which is characteristic of the American nation, and induces them to court hazard or risk, either of life or property, apparently for the sake of overcoming it, has entirely absorbed all great attachment for place or love of home. The associations which gather around this sacred spot, and endear it to the hearts of the people of most nations, is one of slight tenure in the breast of an American. It is true that among the aged, who have spent a long life upon their quiet acres, in the deep bosom of the country, this feeling is still extant, and occasionally one of their more adventurous offspring, who has gone forth in the busy world, and is involved in its cares and perplexities, turns a lingering look towards the old homestead, where his quietest and happiest hours have been passed; but this feeling is but momentary, and is chased away the next instant by some one of the many schemes that take possession of his restless mind.

Occasionally one, in whose breast the recollection of home is more vivid than is usually the case, returns to his native acres and strives to find happiness in maturer years in the contemplation of the scenes of his youth; but it usually happens that the glad spirit which enlivened that period, and beautified every running brook or shady glen, with a coloring of its own, has fled, and in place of the blithesome boy, the care-worn man gazes upon the scenes which once inspired the most delightful emotions with a listless eye and languid look, and wonders how his youthful fancy could have been taken captive by the scenes upon which he now coldly looks, with but little pleasure and much pain. A visit like this too frequently dispels the gay illusion which the man of the world amid his many cares had created for himself, and he returns to the world a wiser but also a sadder man; and if he changes his place of residence, it is to some one further removed than ever from that of his youth, where the associations which he forms are those of the moment.

The great uncertainty of this rule, when applied to such a population as that of the United States, is still further illustrated by a comparison of the average age at death, in the States of Massachusetts and Kentucky. In the former, for a period of five years, ending January 1st, 1854, 92,174 deaths are recorded, whose average age was 26.93 years. In the latter State the recorded deaths, in 1852, amounted to 12,058, with an average age of 20.55 years for the white population, and 17.59 for the colored. During the year 1853, 9,105 occurred, the average ages of which were 20.76 years for the whites, and 18.34 for the colored deaths. Thus—

Massachusetts, for five years, average age at death, . . 26.93 years.
Kentucky, for 1852, white, " " " . . . 20.55 "
" " black, " " " . . . 17.59 "
" for 1853, white, " " " . . . 20.76 "
" " black, " " " . . . 18.34 "

These facts establish pretty clearly the proposition, that the more youthful a country or population is, the less will be its average age at death, provided the proportion of females assimilates pretty nearly to that of the males, as it is the presence and death of the infantile part of the population that reduces the average age at death. In California, where the female portion of the population is greatly in the minority, a high average age at death might be expected; whereas in Indiana, Iowa or Kentucky, it would probably be low, for it is to be taken for granted that in each of the new States the proportion of children to the number of females of a marriageable age is greater than in the older ones.

It will be seen that those populations in the old world and in the new, that remain in the most perfect state of repose, losing perhaps their younger members by emigration, but receiving none of the same age in return, exhibit the highest average age at death. This is evidenced by Geneva, in Switzerland, and Concord, in New Hampshire, both of whose populations are remarkably stationary. Plympton, in Massachusetts, is another evidence of the effect of an aged and stationary population upon the average age at death.

"The whole number of deaths in Plymptom, during thirty years, from January, 1812, to January, 1842, was 218 males, 226 females; total, 443. The average age of all the deceased persons, was 40 years, 10 months, and 25 15-24 days. The average age of the males was 39 years, 9 months, and 9 20-24 days. The average age of the females, was 41 years, 11 months, and 28 8-24 days. There were probably as many people in Plympton, at the commencement of the war of the revolution, as there are now, *i.e.*, 861."*

These illustrations show that the same causes which produce a low average age, either of the living or the dead, operate alike in both hemispheres, and are the peculiar incidents of American life. That a large percentage of infantile mortality will not only depress the average age at death, but also that of the living, is readily admitted; but this is not the only cause competent to produce this result, nor is it always a manifestation of the unhealthiness of a place, and certainly none of its want of prosperity, as is made manifest by a comparison of some quiet town in New England, and an active town in the New States.

---

* Report of Town Clerk.

The annexed table exhibits the average at death in Boston, New York, Philadelphia and Charleston, four cities in different degrees of latitude, situated upon the Atlantic seaboard, and of an age corresponding tolerably well with each other:—

Place and Period.		All Ages.		Under 20.		Over 20.	
		Number.	Average Age.	Number.	Average Age.	Number.	Average Age.
Charleston, 1822 to 1830,	Whites,	3,447	32.63	963	4.62	2,484	43.55
	Blacks,	4,076	28.66	1,950	3.93	2,126	51.33
	Both,	7,523	30.59	2,913	4.16	4,610	47.28
1831 to 1840,	Whites,	3,366	32.65	866	5.14	2,500	43.26
	Blacks,	4,297	30,74	1,957	4.70	2,340	48.24
	Both,	7,663	31.05	2,823	4.88	4,840	45.11
1841 to 1848,	Whites,	1,866	33.41	614	3.68	1,272	47.74
	Blacks,	2,847	28.35	1,416	3.90	1,431	52.56
	Both,	4,733	30.39	2,030	3.83	2,703	50.29
Boston,							
1821 to 1830,	Both,	10,731	25.88	4,913	3.38	5,817	44.88
1831 to 1840,	"	16,314	22.72	8,565	3.33	7,749	44.15
1841 to 1845,	"	10,422	21.43	5,875	3.31	4,547	44.86
New York,							
1821 to 1830,	"	42,817	24.36	20,018	3.15	22,709	43.14
1831 to 1840,	"	74,819	19.46	40,728	2.95	34,091	39.18
1841 to 1843,	"	29,939	19.69	14,127	2.86	10,812	41.68
Philadelphia,							
1821 to 1830,	"	36,614	25.53	17,794	3.22	19,820	45.57
1831 to 1840,	"	49,678	22.64	26,812	2.91	22,866	45.78
1841 to 1844,	"	21,356	22.01	12,088	3.02	9,268	46.79

An examination of this table leaves no room to doubt that New York and Philadelphia were depressed to this low standard, by the great mortality which prevailed in each among the infantile portion of the population. It has already been seen that the infantile period of life was more kindly dealt with in the warm climate of the southern States, and it might reasonably be anticipated that in proportion to the number of inhabitants living of that age, the deaths would be fewer at the south than at the north.

CHAPTER XVI.

GENERAL OBSERVATIONS.

An attempt has been made in the preceding pages to take a comprehensive survey of the vital condition of the population of the whole Union, and, so far as the facts permitted, to pourtray and classify the peculiarities of each section. The materials used in the prosecution of this undertaking, were not all that might be desired, but such as actually existed, and could be commanded. In many instances they have been sufficient not only to lead to suggestions, but also to substantiate them; in others, they have only served the purpose of exciting the mind to the adoption of an inference, without supplying the materials necessary to prosecute it to a final conclusion.

Some of the most apparently important deductions, drawn from scanty and insufficient data, are in this position, and await the accumulation of a sufficient number of facts to prove their correctness, or show their improbability. In no part of the country has the registration of births, deaths and marriages been conducted with sufficient care, and arranged with sufficient precision, to ensure such results as might be desired, with the single exception of the State of Massachusetts, whose labors in this department of enquiry are above all praise.

Climate and latitude are seen to exercise an influence in the production of particular diseases, and in the relative number of deaths at particular ages, too evident not to be admitted, and too important to be overlooked. "The influence of climate," says Dr. Johnson, in his work on Italian climate, "not only on the complexion, but on the features and the whole organization of man, as well as of animals and vegetables, is now unquestioned. The inhabitants of Italy, notwithstanding the unlimited admixture of Gothic, Grecian, African and Asiatic blood, are almost as uniformily naturalized in respect to color, features, and even moral character, as the inhabitants of Spain, Greece, Egypt, Hindostan, or China. It is impossible to attribute this natural stamp, or impress *entirely*, or even principally to race or hereditary descent, in any country, and least of all in Italy, which, from the circumstance of its universal domination at one time, and complete subjugation at another, became an immense human menagerie, where specimens, nay, colonies of every people on the face of the earth, were commixed and blended together *ad infinitum.* Climate, then, assisted by some other physical causes, and many of a moral nature, has effected as homogeneous a people, mental and corporeal, in Italy, as in most other countries."*

Dr. Armstrong, Deputy-Inspector of Hospitals and Fleets, in the English service, says: "So powerful are the effects of external circumstances, that some of the most striking changes have been produced in the human constitution in the course of a few generations, and become permanent. In the West India Islands the white race, descended from the earlier European settlers, as well as those brought from England, in early life, are tall and well proportioned, with great freedom in the joints. In general, however, the chest is less capacious, and the muscles less strongly marked. Pecu-

---

Johnson on Change of Air, p. 225.

liarities are also observed in the greater prominence of the bones of the cheeks and depth of the orbits; the complexion is paler, and the skin cooler. In New South Wales, the descendants of the first settlers exhibit the same peculiarities, although in a less degree.

"The influence of warm climates is apparent after a few years' residence within the tropics. Europeans lose their sanguineous complexions and acquire the power of resisting heat better than the new comer. This power of accommodation to circumstances arises from a corresponding change in the functions of life, and which is usually attributed to the individual having undergone the process of seasoning, a process of which the most vague opinions seem to be entertained. Even within the limited extent of our own country (England) we observe the influence of local situation on comparing the natives of mountainous districts with those of the low country."*

It is stated by Sir James McGregor, Director General of the Army Medical Board, that so great is the influence of climate and surrounding circumstances upon the physical character of the human race, that a corps levied from the agricultural districts of Wales, or the northern counties of England, will last much longer and endure more hardship than one procured from the materials which abound in the manufacturing towns, as Birmingham and Manchester. The effect upon the *physique* by residence in manufacturing towns is particularly striking. Thus, out of 613 men enlisted in Birmingham and its neighborhood, but 238 were approved as fit for service. This permanent deterioration is still further illustrated by the disqualification for those posts requiring a certain standard of size and strength, produced by long residence in the more crowded parts of London. It is said, that of the men from Spitalfields, and other crowded districts in

---

* Armstrong on Climate, p. 8.

London, who apply for situations in the police force, two out of three are rejected, as physically unfit. In further illustration of this point, "it is observed, that in some of the worst conditioned of the town districts, that the positive number of natives of the aboriginal stock continually diminishes, and that the vacancy, as well as the increase, is made up by emigration from healthier districts."*

In regard to the influence of climate in our own country, Dr. Prichard remarks:—"The tall, lank, gaunt, and otherwise remarkable figures of the Virginians, and men of Carolina, are strikingly different from the short, plump, round-faced farmers of the midland counties in England. The race is originally the same, and the deviation in it must be attributed to the influence of the circumstances, whatever they may be, which are connected with local situation."†

All of these authorities, which might be greatly multiplied, are emphatic in their testimony as to the influence of climate over the human organization in a state of health, predisposing it to disease under certain defined circumstances, and preserving it from them under others. The facts collected in the preceding pages demonstrate the extent of this influence in the wide range of latitude and climate embraced within the limits of the United States, "which is," says Maltebrun, "so inconstant and variable, that it passes rapidly from the frosts of Norway to the scorching heats of Africa, and from the humidity of Holland to the drought of Castile."

The effect of climate is greatly modified by long residence, by which means the system undergoes a change fiting it to withstand the deleterious influences that surround it. This process is termed acclimation, and is especially marked in its effect upon the constitution of those who change their

---

* Report of Poor Law Commissioner, 1842.

† Researches into the Physical History of Man, by James Cowles Prichard, vol. 2, p. 563.

residence from a cold to a warm latitude. "Habit," remarks Dr. La Roche, "seems to possess the power of modifying the system to so great an extent, and so permanent a degree, as to justify those who hold it in the light of a second nature. In virtue of the influence it exercises, and the peculiar organic changes resulting from long exposure to the sensible and insensible qualities of the atmosphere, or to the extraneous materials by which the atmosphere may be contaminated, man enjoys the faculty to which I have alluded, of living under climatic influences of the most diversified characters. He resists the inclemencies of the elements, the insalubrity of the seasons, the extremes of temperature, as well as the action of malarial and other exhalations. With time, the native of the north acquires the privilege of supporting with impunity the scorching rays of a tropical sun, though the result is not obtained without inconvenience, suffering, and even danger, and without, in the greater number of instances, subjecting the individual to the ordeal of disease. Not so easy is it to become habituated to the baneful action of those modifiers—such as malarial exhalations—which exercise their agency on the principles of vitality.*

Those who are born in the neighborhood of marshes, are less affected by the miasm arising from them, than new comers, who are almost certain to be attacked by malarial diseases. The American bottom, which is situated in Illinois, contiguous to the Mississippi river, and extends backs to the bluffs, some few miles inland, presents one of the most extensive marshy districts in the United States. The inhabitants of this fertile but miasmatic district, although possessed of a yellow and sallow hue, acquire the power of resisting the miasmatic influence that constantly environs them to a certain extent, while an exposure for a single night to those unaccustomed to the miasm is almost certain to be followed by an attack of fever. It is so

---

* La Roche on Yellow Fever, vol. 2, p. 20.

customary for strangers visiting the more southern parts of the valley of the Mississippi to be attacked by fever, that Dr. Fenner says, "the term acclimation is perfectly well known to all the inhabitants of the lower valley, and indicates that persons coming from a northern climate and settling there, are very liable to have attacks of fever during the first two or three years of their residence, but afterwards become quite exempt."*

Drs. Nott, Dickson, and many other southern medical men who are in the habit of observing the effect of long-continued residence in malarial districts, are of the opinion that the system is rather predisposed to an attack of autumnal fever, by having previously suffered rather than protected by its occurrence. In the malarial districts of Maryland, the writer has had occasion to observe frequent attacks in the same individual, and has known one instance in which a gentleman has suffered from sixteen attacks of remittent fever in seventeen consecutive seasons.

These observations, although applicable with greater force to southern than northern latitudes, are nevertheless general in their application, and extend to all varieties of climate and many modifications of disease. The same laws which modify the temperature, arrange the constituents of the soil, and bestow upon the inanimate objects of creation their peculiar and marked characteristics, also exercise their control over the human system, bestowing upon it peculiarity of color, shape, and powers of endurance, and so modify it as to fit it for the particular situation in which it is placed.

The most fatal disease, however, to those who are unacclimated, is yellow fever, which prevails within the tropics and in the southern cities of the United States. Dr. Barton, in his excellent report on the yellow fever, as it occurred in New Orleans, has a table showing " the life cost of acclimation;

---

* Fenner's Southern Medical Reports, p. 32.

or liabilities to yellow fever from nativity, as exhibited by the epidemic of 1853:"—

NATIVITIES—STATE AND COUNTRY.	Estimated population in 1853.	Estimated mortality from Fever.	Ratio per 1000 of the Population.
New Orleans,	46,004	{ 140	3.58
State of Louisiana,		25	
Arkansas, Mississippi, Alabama, Georgia, South Carolina,	3,176	42	13.22
North Carolina, Virginia, Maryland, Tennessee, Kentucky,	4,984	153	30.09
New York, Vermont, Massachusetts, Maine, Rhode Island, Connecticut, New Jersey, Pennsylvania, Delaware,	10,751	353	32.83
Ohio, Indiana, Illinois, Missouri,	2,030	92	44.23
British America,	381	20	50.24
Totals,	66,946	825	12.32
West Indies, South America, Mexico,	1,790	11	6.14
Great Britain,	4,598	240	52.19
Ireland,	26,611	3,569	204.97
Denmark, Sweden, Russia,	588	96	163.26
Prussia, Germany,	17,718	2,339	132.01
Holland, Belgium,	152	50	328.94
Austria, Switzerland,	797	176	220.08
France,	9,967	480	48.13
Spain, Italy,	2,217	61	22.06
Totals	62,448	7,011	111.91

It is supposed by many that a continued residence in a city where yellow fever is of frequent occurrence, as in Charleston, Savannah, Mobile, or New Orleans, furnishes an entire immunity against its attack. It is extremely doubtful, however, whether any permanent immunity can be obtained which is not based upon an absolute attack of the disease. Dr. Stone, of Charity Hospital, New Orleans, whose experience in yellow fever is large, is clearly of the opinion that the disease must be once taken in order to afford future protection. In a large practice, he has known no one to escape, although he has frequently observed attacks in young children, and even infants, so slight as scarcely to attract the notice of their nurses or parents. Dr. Barton asserts, "*that perfect acclimation is only to be derived from once having had the disease.*" "One of the most extraordinary features of this epidemic," remarks Dr. Fenner, in speaking of the scourge of yellow fever, in 1853, "is presented in the fact, that the natives of the city, both white and colored, have suffered severely, and many of them have died." The same was observed at Charleston, Savannah and Mobile, as well as those towns on the Mississippi river which were visited by the disease. Nor is the immunity extended to those rural districts where it does not prevail. Dr. Dowler, in speaking of the disease as it prevails at Charleston, says: "Those who live in the higher parts of the State, at a distance of two or three hundred miles, and who come to Charleston during the four months in which the yellow fever commonly prevails, are as liable to be attacked by it as strangers; and, therefore, all intercourse between the country and city is suspended for one-third of the year, excepting that of a few white persons, who, from necessity, go to the latter, always taking care, however, not to sleep there."

The table already introduced, showing the relative mortality in New Orleans, in each 1,000, of the inhabitants of different countries, and different sections of this country, exhibits in a very remarkable manner the influence exerted by long residence in a warm climate. Thus among the strangers from the northern portions of the United States, a larger number were attacked than among those from the lower latitudes of Kentucky, Virginia, Tennessee, and North Carolina; and of these latter, a much larger number than from the still lower latitudes of South Carolina, Alabama, Georgia, and Mississippi. The proportions being:

From Northern latitudes, . . . 32.83 per 1,000
" Middle " . . . 30.69 "
" Southern " . . . 13.22 "

In regard to European residents, the same preference for subjects from northern latitudes obtained. While those from Austria, Russia, and Great Britain suffered severely, those from France were less subject to attack, and those from Spain and Italy still less. From this it would appear that a long-continued residence in warm latitudes, even when freed from the causes that produce yellow fever, effects such a modification in the constitution, as to serve in some degree to ward off an attack, and that an eminent predisposition is found in that condition of body, induced by a long residence in a high latitude. That the chances of escape from an attack of yellow fever, when exposed to its influence, by a native of South Carolina or Virginia, are greater than those of a native of Ohio, New York, or the New England States, under like circumstances, appears to be tolerably well established. Did the opportunity exist for obtaining similar information in regard to the diseases which prevail in northern latitudes, in the more inclement season of the year, it would probably be found that the natives of warm latitudes suffered much more in the process of acclimation than is generally supposed, and that modifications of habit, equally important with those already noticed, are necessary, in order to enable the southern resident to withstand the depressing effects of cold.

That these alternations of temperature exert a powerful influence over the human organization, and that a continued residence either amid the snows of the frigid zone, or the burning heat of the equatorial region, produces such modifications as to render a sudden transition from the one to the other a matter of extreme hazard, cannot be questioned. Not only the facts set forth in the preceding pages, but the concurrent testimony of nearly all accurate observers, goes to show, that independent of all local circumstances, the heat of low latitudes is sufficient to induce a train of affections peculiar to and dependent on a warm climate, while cold, on the contrary, is attended with those peculiar to northern regions.

"Fever, dysentery, liver disease in some shape, with every variety of bowel affections, may be regarded as the diseases of hot climates. Cold, on the other hand, when inordinate or sudden, arrests the subcutaneous circulation, retards secretion and colorification, and drives the blood from the skin, which becomes rough to the interior, where it circulates sluggishly and in large quantities. The natural effect of this derangement of these important functions is to induce inflammatory or sub-inflammatory affections, especially of those parts which are most engorged. Hence, inflammation of the mucous membrane of the air-passages—cough and bronchitis—are especially induced by sudden or extreme cold."* An examination of the causes of death in different latitudes, as developed in this report, will demonstrate how generally affections of one or the other of these classes are amenable to the influence of elevated and depressed temperature, and how important a feature they constitute in the medical history of the country. In England the winter months are invariably the most fatal, while in the United States they are usually among the most healthy. In regard to the effect upon aged persons, the winter of England and that of the United States presents a fair parallel.

A remarkable instance of the effect of long-continued cold upon the human system is found in the case of Dr. Kane and his companions in their recent search in the Polar regions for the ill-fated expedition of Sir John Franklin. Upon the return of Dr. Kane and his party from their residence of three years in a high northern latitude, they found that the effect of summer heat in a northern climate was so depressing as to produce extreme

---

* Dunglison's Human Health, p. 27.

nervous prostration, and unfit them for mental or corporeal exertion. In the case of Dr. Kane, this nervous prostration was so great, as absolutely to destroy all power of physical endurance, and finally resulted in his death.

The effect of age is important. In those affections which are dependent upon an increased excitability of the system, as in all the diseases induced by warm climates, the middle period of life is that in which they prove most fatal; while those diseases which are induced by a diminution of this excitability, as in the case of those due exclusively to a cold climate, old age, or an impaired vitality, are least favorable to recovery.

The effect of this diversity of climate and surrounding circumstances upon the relative prevalence of the one or the other of the diseases to which each are subject, and the comparative duration of life, has been fully recognised by those whose duty it is to apply the laws of mortality, either known or supposed, to the operations of life assurance. Experience has demonstrated to those companies having risks in different countries or in different climates in the same country, that the percentage of mortality, under apparently like circumstances, is greater in some situations than in others, and that what might be a profitable rate in one would be a losing rate in the other.

The annexed table, showing the combined results of the operations of the order of Odd Fellows in the United States, for ten years, commencing with 1843, and ending with 1852, is highly pertinent to this subject, and illustrates, in the most marked manner, the influence of locality upon health and disease. This table derives additional value from the circumstance that the Odd Fellows were for the most part like those who seek assurance in the middle period of life :—

STATISTICS OF MORTALITY

State Grand Lodges.	Beneficial Members.	Number Sick.	Ratio Sick.	Number Deaths.	One death to each
Maryland,	59,131	13,021	4.5	641	92
Massachusetts,	78,711	9,892	7.9	659	119
S. New York,	161,742	28,818	5.6	1,733	93
N. New York,	93,142	14,662	6.3	653	142
Pennsylvania,	204,689	37,150	5.5	1,829	111
District Columbia,	10,398	2,458	5.2	77	135
Delaware,	7,800	1,016	7.3	61	127
Ohio,	59,673	9,973	5.9	639	93
Louisiana,	9,924	1,110	8.6	211	47
New Jersey,	42,671	6,989	6.1	322	132
Kentucky,	17,561	2,197	7.9	243	72
Virginia,	31,048	4,824	6.4	336	92
Indiana,	17,981	2,582	6.9	203	88
Mississippi,	8,266	816	10.1	89	92
Missouri,	10,988	1,446	7.6	187	58
Illinois,	14,339	1,613	8.3	162	88
Texas,	1,340	139	8.2	34	39
Alabama,	7,469	725	10.3	119	63
Connecticut,	37,713	5,843	6.4	273	138
South Carolina,	13,812	1,518	9.0	128	107
Tennessee,	11,918	860	13.3	93	128
Georgia,	11,768	1,403	8.3	134	87
North Carolina,	6,710	645	9.8	59	113
Maine,	33,138	3,543	9.3	271	122
Rhode Island,	9,621	1,537	6.2	78	123
New Hampshire,	14,454	1,812	7.9	120	120
Michigan,	14,341	2,077	6.9	111	129
Wisconsin,	9,099	625	11.8	58	156
Vermont,	4,785	490	8.2	27	177
Iowa,	4,380	425	7.9	36	121
	1,008,612	160,209	6.3	9,586	105

This table would have derived an additional value if it had contained the ages at death, and the occupations of the deceased. This latter enquiry, whose importance is of the highest value in measuring the relative duration of life, has latterly received much attention at home and abroad. It unfortunately happens, however, that the European observations are mainly confined to England and Scotland, and those in this country to the States of Massachusetts and Rhode Island.

Mr. Neison, the Actuary of the Medical Invalid and General Life Office, at London, obtained, after much labor, the results of a sufficient number of Friendly Societies, whose province is to provide for the sick, to enable him to institute a comparison into the relative health of the various occupations included in the returns, and the comparative healthfulness of each in town and country districts. This enables a comparison to be made between the returns of the occupations, as found in the Massachusetts reports, and those of similar occupations in England. It is much to be regretted that no extensive means of comparison with the records of Massachusetts, is to be found at home, the only State which has noted the occupations of the deceased being the neighboring one of Rhode Island, and the whole number of occupations so noted being confined to less than two hundred deaths.

The results of Mr. Neison's investigations disclosed the fact, that notwithstanding the circumstances which at the first view might be supposed to exercise a very large influence in abridging life, the members of Friendly Societies were longer lived than the average residents of the same districts of similar ages, although a large number of these latter were among the affluent classes of society, who from their greater comforts and limited exposure, were supposed to present a higher average age at death than their more humble neighbors.

The data collected from the Friendly Societies was carefully arranged in three classes, dependent upon the residence of the members, viz., town, city and country, in order to test the effect of locality upon the life of persons pursuing the same occupation under the different circumstances of town and country life. These were grouped together, and a table of the expectation of life, formed from the results, and contrasted with the expectation of life among the males in England and Wales for the same periods. This table, which is given below, shows that at each age the expectation of life is invariably in favor of the members of the Friendly Societies, and speaks in very encouraging language to those whose province it is to toil at laborious and frequently dangerous occupations :—

Age.	Expectation in		Difference in Favor of the Three Districts.	
	Three Districts.	England and Wales.	In Years.	Per Cent.
20	43.77	40.69	3.08	7.57
30	36.60	34.09	2.50	7.34
40	29.33	27.47	1.85	6.75
50	22.19	20.84	1.34	6.45
60	15.69	14.58	1.10	7.60
70	10.20	9.21	0.98	10.72

These results, so far showing that the circumstances in which the laborious classes are placed limit their duration of life, absolutely exhibits a prolongation of it beyond what the most favorable life tables, selected from the best classes of society, have ventured to go, and excited much surprise among those who were by no means ignorant on this subject.

But although the average was more favorable to life than that of the whole population, yet a large difference was found to obtain in the relative healthfulness of different occupations, as will be made manifest by the following table :—

AMONG MEMBERS OF FRIENDLY SOCIETIES.

Ages.	Rural, Town, and City Districts. G.	Clerks. J, No. 2.	Plumbers, Painters, and Glaziers. J, No. 3.	Bakers. J, No. 4.	Miners. J, No. 5.
20	43.77	31.83	36.90	40.02	40.67
30	36.60	27.57	30.50	32.35	33.15
40	29.33	21.85	24.30	24.47	24.92
50	22.19	16.04	17.09	19.09	17.53
60	15.69	12.42	12.16	14.06	11.85

From this it appears that the expectation of life at twenty years for all trades included in the Friendly Societies, is 43.77 years; for miners alone, 40.67 years; for bakers, 40 years; for painters, plumbers and glaziers, 36.90 years; and for clerks, the low average of 31.83 years.

"The very remarkable difference," adds Mr. Neison, "between the above employments and the general results, cannot fail to occasion some surprise; and at the same time conclusively prove, that any district containing a majority of the above, or other equally unhealthy employments, must show a very reduced average value of life for the district, independent of the local situation itself on health."*

The Massachusetts returns not only embrace those usually included in Friendly Societies abroad or at home, but also those on the one hand in the latter classes whose means are abundant and exposure little; and on the other, who derive their sustenance from the hand of charity.

The following table exhibits the most common occupations of those who have died in Massachusetts during eleven years and eight months, ending on the last day of December, 1854, together with the average age that has been attained by the deceased, in each of the selected occupations:—

---

* Journal London Statistical Society, vol. 8, p. 313.

No.		Age.	No.		Age.
9698	Agriculturists,	47.16	359	Masons,	41.61
29	Artists,	40.10	408	Mechanics,	42.88
11	Bank Officers,	61.72	816	Merchants,	52.06
688	Blacksmiths,	51.41	69	Millers,	61.58
124	Butchers,	49.63	50	Musicians,	40.46
198	Cabinetmakers,	47.04	260	Operatives,	34.19
1498	Carpenters,	49.33	368	Painters,	42.10
234	Clergymen,	56.61	356	Paupers,	65.19
437	Clerks,	33.73	322	Physicians,	55.25
286	Coopers,	58.84	129	Printers,	36.55
263	Gentlemen,	63.83	80	Ropemakers,	55.95
21	Glass Blowers,	39.86	2299	Seamen,	45.99
111	Hatters,	54.90	238	Shipwrights,	56.48
7	Judges and Justices,	67.19	2436	Shoemakers,	43.66
92	Jewelers,	42.56	194	Stonecutters,	43.66
6410	Laborers,	44.57	287	Tailors,	42.51
171	Lawyers,	56.60	175	Tanners and Curriers,	47.37
363	Machinists,	37.63	648	Traders,	46.53
313	Manufacturers,	44.30	95	Weavers,	46.83

"Of these 33,580 individuals the combined ages amounted to 1,724,031 years, or 51.34 years to each man.

"A portion of the females who died during the same time, admit of the following classification:—

Domestics,	43.96	Seamstresses,	41.83
Dressmakers,	32.36	Shoebinders,	45.59
Housekeepers,	51.15	Straw-braiders,	35.09
Milliners,	35.53	Tailoresses,	40.63
Nurses,	54.61	Teachers,	28.70
Operatives,	27.69		

"The aggregate ages of the 2,376 females thus given, amounted to 109,724, and the general average of the whole gives 50.39 years to each individual.

DIFFERENT OCCUPATIONS.

The Registrar of the city of Boston has furnished the following table of ages of 706 men, of the principal professions and trades, who died in 1855, and whose ages were reported:—

No.	Profession or Occupation.	Ages Ranging from	Aggregate Ages.	Average Ages.
305	Laborers,	16 to 88	12,292	40.30
69	Mariners,	16 " 79	2,663	38.59
45	Clerks,	16 " 74	1,484	32.98
35	Tailors,	20 " 90	1,368	39.08
32	Merchants,	26 " 91	1,882	58.81
32	Traders,	24 " 79	1,590	49.68
33	Carpenters,	18 " 87	1,510	45.76
22	Painters,	19 " 76	888	40.36
20	Shoemakers,	21 " 55	687	34.35
15	Teamsters,	22 " 73	516	34.40
12	Gentlemen,	28 " 83	718	59.83
11	Printers,	20 " 68	434	39.45
10	Masons,	25 " 71	402	40.20
9	Machinists,	23 " 46	304	33.77
8	Bakers,	26 " 60	309	38.62
8	Farmers,	35 " 71	457	57.12
7	Blacksmiths,	20 " 58	245	35.00
6	Ship Carpenters,	30 " 70	307	51.16
5	Physicians,	25 " 72	249	49.80
5	Clergymen,	36 " 73	269	53.80
4	Coopers,	26 " 55	162	40.50
4	Curriers,	19 " 40	114	28.50
4	Engineers,	27 " 54	183	45.75
5	Lawyers,	27 " 91	301	60.20
706	Totals,	..	29,334	41.55

There is no absolute means of separating those who resided in town from those who lived in the country, but it is presumed that the agriculturists were exclusively residents of the country; while it is probable that the larger part of those classed under the heads of mechanics and laborers dwelt in towns of greater or less size. The effect of locality, upon this presumption, is made strikingly manifest in the superior value of life possessed by the agriculturist over that of the two classes of laborers who reside in town, being eighteen years longer in duration than that of the mechanic, and nearly twenty years beyond that of the laborer.

These observations correspond somewhat with those of Mr. Neison's, which value the probabilities of the life of the baker below the average of mechanics, the life of the painter still lower, and that of the clerk lowest of all the occupations. They cannot be pursued further, because Mr. Neison has not given the probabilities of life incident to the other trades that came under his inspection, but they are sufficient to show that under like circumstances the relative probabilities of life, as compared the one with the other, do not differ materially in England and Massachusetts.

This classification shows a very marked difference in the average age at death of the different mechanic arts, besides those just alluded to. Tanners and curriers, butchers and carpenters, stand high upon the list; while machinists, and stonecutters, and printers, take a low stand. This table is very valuable so far as it goes, but it fails to enumerate many occupations more unhealthy than those already named, as the white lead manufacturer, the friction-matchmaker, and the daguerreotypist.

There are obvious reasons, growing out of the circumstances incident to each pursuit, why one should be more favorable to longevity than another; and were the diseases in each case carefully noted, it would lead to very satisfactory and practical results.

In 1819, the English Government selected Mr. Finlaison, an eminent mathematician and vital statistician, to determine the law of mortality, and establish the value of the government annuities, and tontine schemes. Assisted by a large number of competent clerks, and aided by access to the records of the names of those who for the space of a century had been upon the registers, as the recipients of annuities, or the nominees in tontines, and also provided with unlimited means to defray any expenditure required in the prosecution of his inquiries, he labored assiduously at his task, and at the expiration of ten years made a final report to the Lords of the Treasury, which comprised in a large number of tables the rates of mortality, and the value of a great number of different classes of annuities averaged for single and more lives.

These tables, thus laboriously wrought out with consummate skill and great care, are regarded as the true exponent of the expectation of life in the class covered by his inquiries, and have always commanded the fullest confidence.

From a comparison of the data furnished by them, as well as that collected by the various assurance companies, it appeared that the value of life among the government annuitants, and the insurers of lives in the different assurance companies, which represented the affluent and superior classes, was less, as has already been observed, than among the humbler classes, found among the members of Friendly Societies.

Dr. Guy, of King's College Hospital, from the facts afforded him by the works on peerage and baronetage, made a classification of the deaths which had occurred among the members of noble families, above twenty years of age, for a long period of years.

The number of deaths thus collated amount to 2291, of which 1989 were derived from the peerage, and the remainder from the baronetage. From these facts Mr. Neison formed a life table, showing the expectation of life in the males of the peerage and baronetage.

The expectation of life, as thus deduced, together with the results obtained by Mr. Finlaison, on English annuitants, the experience of several assurance companies, Milne's and Farr's tables, and that of the French annuitants, are placed side by side in the accompanying table:—

Age.	Peerage and Bart.	England (Mr. Farr.)	English Ann. (Finlaison.)	Sweden & Finland, (Milne.)	Carlisle, (Milne.)	Equitable, (Morgan.)	Amicable, (Galloway)	French Ann. (Depar.)
20	38	40	38	39	41	42	..	40
25	35	36	36	35	38	38	38	37
30	31	33	33	32	34	34	34	34
35	27	30	30	28	31	31	30	31
40	24	27	27	25	28	27	26	27
45	21	23	24	21	24	24	22	24
50	18	20	20	18	21	20	19	20
55	15	17	17	15	18	17	16	17
60	13	14	14	12	14	14	13	14
65	10	11	12	10	12	11	10	11
70	8	8	9	7	9	9	8	9
75	6	6	7	5	7	7	6	6
80	5	5	5	4	5	5	5	5
85	4	4	3	3	4	3	4	3
90	3	3	2	3	3	3	3	2
95	2	2	.	2	3	.	.	.
100	1	.	.	.	.	.	.	.

These columns certainly do not exhibit as high an expectation of life, either among the members of the families of the peerage and baronetage, or the English annuitants, as the average of English life shown in the column based upon Mr. Farr's results, and all of these fall below that of Mr. Neison's, based upon the facts developed by the returns of the Friendly Societies.

A comparison of the laboring and more independent classes in the United States, as developed by the Massachusetts returns, do not exhibit the same favorable results for the former, as are made manifest by the English tables. On the contrary, the average age at death of those engaged in mechanical pursuits is lower than the average age of the better classes.

The average age of laborers is 44.80 years, and that of mechanics as a class 46 years, while with merchants, the average age is 46.30 years, with professional men 49.03 years, and with public men 50.32 years. Among individual pursuits, those of the clergymen, advocates and medical men, rank higher than either of the trades, with the exception of the cooper and the shipwright, and the retired gentleman attains to an age superior to them all, averaging 68.29 years.

There is a very wide difference between the relative chances of life enjoyed by the different classes in Massachusetts and England, which must arise either from the higher expectation of life among the better class here, as compared with the same class in England, or a lower expectation among the laboring class here, as compared with the same class there.

In applying the principles of the laws of mortality to life assurance, it must be taken into consideration, that while a knowledge of their rates at the extreme periods of life is necessary, yet at the same time those circumstances which affect its duration after the first period has passed, and extreme age has not been attained, are of more immediate and practical importance, because it is precisely in this period of life that most applicants for assurance present themselves, and over which most of the policies, whose duration is limited by a fixed number of years extend. It may thus happen that the proportionate mortality of one latitude may not exceed that of another, or may even fall below; and yet the probabilities of life at the ages usually covered by life assurance may be much less. Thus, if the prevailing disease be dysentery or scarlatina, its heaviest demand will be made upon the early periods of life; if consumption and scrofula, it will fall with greatest force upon the period between 20 and 30 years; and if dropsy, apoplexy, or paralysis, it will fall with greatest force upon advanced life.

In order, therefore, to determine with any degree of accuracy the effect of locality upon the duration of life, a knowledge of the diseases that terminate it is as necessary as an exact account of the number who have died, and the ages at which death took place. The tables accompanying this report will, it is hoped, enable these comparisons to be instituted with a reasonable approximation to correct results.

WM. C. BRYANT & CO., PRINTERS, CORNER NASSAU AND LIBERTY STREETS, N. Y.

INDEX.

	PAGE
Acclimation,	171
"	196
" Dr. La Roche on	197
" Life, cost of	199
" Dr. Nott on	198
Age of parents, effect on sexes at births,	76
Ages of living in each State,	181
" at marriage in Massachusetts,	92
" " " " Kentucky,	93
" " " " Belgium,	93
" " " " North and South,	96
Aged class of population,	33
American summer, heat of	136
" " source of disease,	136
Army mortality in British service,	131
" " " United States,	133
" statistics not applicable to civil life,	134
Atlantic plain, features of	137
Average age of English population,	32
" " " American "	32
" " " at death,	183
Balfour, Dr., on table of mortality in Eastern British service,	131
Births, census returns of	45
" disparity in	45
" why greater in some places than others,	45

	PAGE
Births, more abundant in new than old countries,	45
" affected by the seasons,	49
" Milne on	48
" in Massachusetts,	58
" in Rhode Island,	59
" in New Jersey,	63
" in Connecticut,	63
" in Kentucky,	64
Born dead, proportion of	77
" " " in Kentucky,	78
" " " in Massachusetts,	77
" " " in European countries,	79
Boston, births in	55
" " of natives and foreigners,	56
" " in different wards,	56
" " mortality in	164
Bowditch, Dr., on consumption in Massachusetts,	178
California, mortality	160
Carpenter on sexes at birth,	76
Carnival, effect of on season of marriage in France,	91
Chadwick on population in United States,	31
" " average age of living,	32
Chickering on Emigration,	43

INDEX.

	PAGE
Census returns of births,	103
" " " marriages,	103
" " " deaths,	107
Climate of the great lake region,	144
" " mountain "	144
" " sea shore and inland,	194
" Dr. Johnson on	494
Clark, Dr., on still-born,	81
Conception in Kentucky,	83
" effect of seasons on	83
" Milne on	84
" in Sweden and France,	85
Connecticut, births in	63
Consumption, season most fatal,	176
" in Massachusetts,	178
" in Kentucky,	177
" Dr. Bowditch on	178
" per cent. of, in Massachusetts and Kentucky,	180
Curtis, Dr., on sexes at birth,	67
Deaths, census returns of	107
" in different States,	107
" number of in United States,	107
" proportion of sexes,	108
" in Massachusetts,	108
" in New Hampshire,	108
" per cent. at different ages,	109
" excess of males in early life,	110
" proportion to living,	110
" male and female in Massachusetts,	111
" " " Dist. of Columbia,	111
" " " Wurtemberg,	111
" affected by migration,	113
" in each season,	151
" different States,	151
Dependent classes,	33
Diseases, classification of	172
" of warm climates,	202
" of cold "	202
" per cent. of, in different States,	175
" " " " localities,	179
Drake, Dr., on Mississippi Valley,	19

	PAGE
Dwellings, number of in Europe,	156
" " " in United States,	155
Effect of locality on mortality,	164
" " geological formation on health,	141
Emigration, per cent. in United States,	39
" " " " different States,	39
" " " " European countries,	41
" Irish to America,	52
Emigrants, condition of	41
" now and heretofore,	43
" in town and country,	40
Emigrant office, English, report of	53
European States, births in	65
Fecundity, laws of	48
Females, deaths among	108
" " in Massachusetts,	110
" " in Dist. of Columbia,	110
" " in Wurtemberg,	111
" " in excess in country,	115
Female mortality in Massachusetts,	125
" " in Maryland,	125
" " in England,	125
Fever, a disease of middle life,	179
" per cent. of, in Massachusetts and Kentucky,	180
Finlaison on English Annuitants,	180
Gotha Bank do not insure pregnant women,	122
Geology of the Atlantic plain and slope,	137
" of Valley of Mississippi,	140
Gulf stream, effect of	147
Guy, Dr., on lives of English peerage,	211
Hofacker on sexes at birth,	76
Hopfs' statistics of male and female mortality,	122
Heat of American summer a source of disease,	135
Ireland, marriages in	50
" proportion of births,	50

INDEX.

	PAGE
Ireland, Thom's statistics	53
Irish condition of in Ireland and America,	52
Infantile mortality,	57
" " excess of	184
" " census returns,	184
" " want of correctness in,	184
Kentucky, births in	64
" still-born in	81
" conception in	83
" months most prolific in	83
" and Montpellier correspondence,	86
Kennedy's table of male and female mortality,	125
Kane, Dr., effect of cold climate on,	203
Life-table, English	13
" insurance experience in male and female mortality,	122
Local influences, effect of	129
Laws of mortality not alike in England and America,	153
Louisiana, Dr. Barton on	168
Locality, effect of on mortality,	178
Mississippi Valley,	19
Mountain ranges,	20
Mortality census,	16
Mortality returns,	25
" of Europe,	25
" per cent. of ,	25
Milne on Conception,	48
Massachusetts, reports of births,	56
Male and female, proportions of in the United States,	75
Massachusetts and Sweden, correspondence between	86
Marriages, in different months	88
" Massachusetts,	83
" Kentucky,	89
" Shattuck on	90
" in different States,	103
" census returns of	103
" proportion of, in different States	103
Moisture, sources of	147

	PAGE
Moisture in Europe and American climates,	147
Mortality in different States,	107
" of the sexes in Massachusetts,	121
" " " at different ages,	121
" correspondence between Sweden and Massachusetts,	128
" among British troops,	131
" maximum and minimum periods of	158
" in Massachusetts,	158
" in Kentucky,	158
" in Rhode Island,	159
" in California,	160
" in Northern and Southern cities,	164
" in Southern States, Dr. Nott on	170
Mourgue on marriages in France,	91
New Jersey, births in	63
New Orleans, Dr. Simonds on the mortality of	165
" Dr. Barton " "	168
Nott, Dr., on mortality of Southern States	170
Neison on effect of occupation,	205
" on select lives	205
Occupation, effect on life	205
" in other countries,	208
" in England,	206
" Deaths in each	208
Odd Fellows, table of mortality among	203
Population of United States,	21
" ages of	21
" distribution of	21
" ratios of each age	21
" origin of	22
" productive capacity of	31
Probabilities of life,	26
Productive classes,	33
Prussian Government's providence,	35
Proportion of sexes at birth,	67
" of males to females in the U. S.	75
Parallelisms in U. States and Europe,	133

INDEX.

	PAGE
Per cent. of mortality in the chief cities of the United States,	164
Quetelet on male and female deaths,	117
" the mortality of the sexes at different ages,	121
Registration among the ancients	10
" in Geneva, Switzerland,	11
" in England,	12
" in United States,	12
" in Massachusetts,	12
" in New Jersey,	13
" in Connecticut,	13
" in Rhode Island,	13
" in Kentucky,	13
" in Virginia,	13
" in South Carolina,	13
Rhode Island, births in	59
Rate of mortality in different countries,	132
" " in U. S. Army,	133
States, areas of	19
" per cent. of area,	19
" ratio of	19
Sexes, proportion of at birth,	67
" " in Massachusetts,	68
" " in Providence,	71
" " in Europe,	70
" " in Kentucky,	72
" " in Virginia,	72
" " in Charleston, S. C.	73
Sadler on sexes at birth,	76
Still-born, properties of	77
Seasons, effect on conception in Kentucky,	83
Sutton, Dr., on conception in Kentucky,	83
Sweden, table of conception in	85
Shattuck on New England marriages,	90
Sardinia, returns of males and females,	118
" returns of male and female deaths in town and country,	120
Sutton's table of mortality of sexes in Kentucky,	125
Seasons in the United States,	135
" influence of	151
" deaths in each	11
Summer mortality in the United States,	152
Sanger, Dr., on mortality of California,	160
Simonds on the mortality of New Orleans,	160
Southwestern mortality	170
Southern mortality greatest in middle life,	180
" " in infancy and old age,	180
Summer mortality in United States,	202
Tucker on probabilities of life,	26
" on mortality in the United States,	26
Thom's Irish statistics,	53
Tripe on still-born,	80
Table of mortality among British troops,	131
" " " in U. S. Army,	133
Temperature, range of in the U. States,	192
" sea and inland,	192
Trade wind, its influence,	147
Town and Country mortality in England and America,	154
Table of per cent. of living of each age in the various States,	181
United States territorial limits,	18
" great divisions,	19
" growth of	23
" natural divisions of	137
" proportion of town and country population	155
Virginia, births in	64
" still-born in	81
Value of European lives, table of	206
Wargentin on still-born,	81
Winds in United States,	135
Winter, mortality in Europe	135
" " in England,	202

NEW YORK:
WM. C. BRYANT & CO., PRINTERS, 41 NASSAU STREET, CORNER OF LIBERTY.

1857.

Printed in Dunstable, United Kingdom